Cambridge checkpoint

Lower Secondary World English

8

Fiona Macgregor
Daphne Paizee
EDUCATIONAL CONSULTANT:
Sioban Parker

HODDER EDUCATION
AN HACHETTE UK COMPANY

Orders: please contact Hachette Uk Distribution, Hely Hutchinson Centre, Milton Road, Didcot, Oxfordshire OX11 7HH. Telephone: +44 (0)1235 827827. Email: education@hachette.co.uk Lines are open from 9 a.m. to 5 p.m., Monday to Friday. You can also order through our website: www.hoddereducation.com

ISBN: 978 1 3983 1142 8

First published in 2021 by
Hodder Education
An Hachette UK Company
Carmelite House
50 Victoria Embankment
London EC4Y 0DZ
www.hoddereducation.com

Impression number 10 9 8 7 6 5 4

Year 2025 2024

Cover © galika - stock.adobe.com

Illustrations by Barking Dog Art, The Bright Agency

Typeset in FS Albert 12/14pt by Ian Foulis Design, Saltash, Cornwall

Printed and bound in Great Britain by Bell & Bain Ltd, Glasgow

A catalogue record for this title is available from the British Library.

FSC www.fsc.org
MIX
Paper | Supporting responsible forestry
FSC™ C104740

Contents

Introduction

How can English help you in your everyday life and **connect** you to the exciting and challenging world in which we live? In *Checkpoint* we encourage you to connect to this world by thinking and reflecting as you learn.

We have provided topics for a variety of different interests, from living in remote areas to using social media and making business plans. You will have the opportunity to use the new language that you learn to **share** ideas and learn from others too. This will help you to become confident and **fluent** in English. The language and the skills that you learn will also help you in other subjects.

Checkpoint therefore helps you to access your world and to stay connected to it. Be the best that you can and become a responsible and thinking citizen of the world.

Enjoy your learning experience!

Daphne Paizee and Fiona Macgregor

How to use this book

To make your study of Cambridge Lower Secondary World English as rewarding as possible, look out for the following features when you are using this book.

- These aims show you what you will be covering in the unit.

PRACTISE

Activities that help you to put new skills, information and knowledge to practical use.

Try this

These questions help you to develop skills, knowledge and comprehension.

CHALLENGE YOURSELF

These are more demanding tasks or tasks that help you to practise a wider range of skills.

Do you remember?

These provide a quick recap on earlier grammar points and may sometimes include a question.

LET'S TALK
These tasks provide opportunities for more free discussion.

DID YOU KNOW?
These contain interesting information or facts.

HINT
Useful points to note or help with an activity.

Self check

Summary questions or tasks that occur at the end of each unit.

What can you do?

This provides an end-of-unit checklist of key content.

This book contains lots of activities to help you learn. Most of these have symbols beside them to help you know what type of activity they are.

Signals a listening activity, along with an audio track reference.

Signals a speaking activity (these are different to the Let's Talk boxes, which are freer discussion tasks that usually occur towards the end of a unit).

This tells you that content is related to another subject.

This tells you that the activities and text relate to the end-of-unit project in Unit 9.

There is a link to digital content at the end of each unit if you are using the Boost eBook.

At the end of this book you will find some additional features to help you while you study.

- The glossary is a list of some words you might not have encountered before, or words that are specific to one of the units you will be studying. If you want to check the meaning of a word you come across in this book, check the glossary. If it's not there, use a dictionary.
- The grammar section includes all the grammar points you will learn throughout this book. It is arranged in alphabetical order so you can find everything easily.
- Check the punctuation chart to remind yourself how to use punctuation accurately in your own writing. This chart will help you understand different forms of punctuation and how to use them properly.
- The pronunciation word bank is a list of interesting words that appear in this book. You might not have heard some of these words before. Listen to the Audio list of these words to learn to pronounce them properly. Read the words as you listen.
- At the back of the book is a list of books you might like to read for enjoyment. Reading is a great way to relax, to use your imagination, and to learn about new people, places and things. Most of all – it's fun!

Enjoy your learning journey.

1 Talking the talk

In this unit you will:

- listen to a radio interview, a song and a podcast about speaking English
- talk about being **bilingual** and speaking different languages
- read infographics about English, a personal **anecdote** about language and stories about language mix-ups
- write a narrative essay and design a poster
- use pronouns, the second conditional, and various question forms to discuss language.

▲ How many different types of English are there in the world? How do you greet your friends and family?

Speaking and listening

My home language

1 Work in your group. Talk about the graphics and the questions on the opposite page.
   a How many people in your group speak English at home?
   b What other languages does each family speak at home?
   c Which language do you like to speak best? Can you explain why?

2 Listen to Manuela talk about her family in Audio 1.1.
As you listen, find the answers to these questions.
   a What languages does Manuela speak?
   b Who speaks English in her family?
   c What is her abuela's attitude towards speaking English?
   d When does her father speak French?
   e Why does her brother want to learn English?

▲ That's me, Manuela, with my abuelo, my abuela, my parents and my brother

HINT

'Abuela' is the Spanish word for 'grandmother' and 'abuelo' is the word for 'grandfather'.

Can you say 'grandmother' and 'grandfather' in any other languages?

Vocabulary

PRACTISE

Have a dialogue with your partner. Ask each other questions about what languages you speak. Use this question frame to help you.

Question: What languages do you speak?

Answer: I speak ...

Question: Do your parents also speak ...?

Answer: Yes/no, they speak ...

Question: What other languages would you like to learn?

Answer: I would like to learn ...

Try this

Can you match these phrases to their meanings in the speech bubbles?

Mother tongue   Second language   Foreign language

A language from another country, which you learn, and which you do not speak at home, or in your community

The language you learn as your first language, from your parents or guardians

Another language that you speak and understand well, that may be spoken in your home or in your community

Speaking and listening

Listen to a radio interview

Listen to Audio 1.2, a radio programme about bilingual people and the **benefits** of speaking more than one language. The interviewer is speaking to Leonie Applegate, a language researcher who specialises in bilingual studies.

Discuss the radio programme in your group. Choose the correct answer in brackets to complete each sentence.

1 Bilingual means (speaking two languages/having more than one official language/living with a lingual).
2 Around the world, more than (40/60/80) per cent of people are bilingual.
3 Most countries have (one/two/more than one) official language.
4 Speaking fluently means (speaking the language Fluent/being able to express yourself in a language without difficulty/speaking two languages).
5 If you speak another language you (can get a job/begin to understand another culture/think differently).
6 Bilingual people have denser brain tissue, because they (are cleverer than **monolingual** people/have to work very hard to think/have to continually filter out one language in order to use the other).

▲ Leonie discusses bilingual learning with the interviewer

DID YOU KNOW?

Bi- means two, and mono- means one. So, bilingual means a person speaks two languages and monolingual means a person speaks only one language. What do you think being trilingual means?

PRACTISE

1 Work with a partner. Use these structures, and your new vocabulary, to make sentences about speaking other languages.

If I spoke Spanish/Arabic/French, I would be ...

If we spoke another language, we would ...

If I was fluent in ..., I would ...

2 Now write down three sentences of your own, using those structures.

3 Practise saying these words out loud. Make sure you emphasise the correct syllable (underlined). Then learn to spell the words.

benefit bilingual monolingual language culture fluent

Being bilingual

DID YOU KNOW?

Not everyone speaks about the world in the same way. In Russia, there are different words for blue. Light blue is seen as a completely different colour from dark blue. The Inuit people in Alaska have over 50 words for snow, from 'snow that is falling softly' to 'snow that is good for driving a sled on'.

LET'S TALK

What other languages do you speak? Discuss this in your group.

- What is your **home language**, or mother tongue?
- Are you bilingual? Which two languages do you speak?
- Do you ever mix up words in the two languages? Why or why not?
- Do you speak about different topics in different languages? For example, do you express emotion in one language, but talk about school in another?
- Is the language you speak at home different from the one you speak outside the home? Why is that?

Try this

In your group, talk about these photographs.

- Describe the colour of the sea. What colour is the sky? Are you sure?
- What colour is the snow? Is it only one colour?
- What words do you know in other languages to describe the colour of the sea, the sky and the snow?

Make a list in your group, then compare your group's list with the rest of the class.

CHALLENGE YOURSELF

Read the paragraph below. Fill in the **gaps** using words from the box. (You can use some words more than once.)

Mother tongue	Russian	Polish	English

My __________ __________ is __________, but my cousins are Polish, so I also speak __________, and we live in London, so we also speak __________. When I talk to my cousins in English, I will sometimes use __________ words, but never Polish words. When I speak to my aunt in Polish, I never introduce __________ words, because she doesn't understand them. I don't have to think about this, it just comes naturally!

Use of English

Pronouns

▲ My French teacher comes from Dijon. She speaks French and also Italian

Do you remember?

Pronouns replace nouns, so you don't have to keep repeating the noun. For example:

> My French teacher comes from Dijon. She also speaks Italian.
>
> My uncle, my aunt and all my cousins speak Mandarin because my uncle worked in Dailan. They speak Mandarin when they don't want us to understand what they are saying!

Subject pronouns are I, he, she, it, you, we, they.

Object pronouns are me, him, her, it, you, us, them.

PRACTISE

1 Can you find the pronouns in this paragraph? Write them down.

> My mother is from Switzerland, where they have four official languages, and she speaks two of them fluently. That has been a huge **advantage** to her. Speaking another language is a good way to begin to understand another culture.

2 Complete these sentences by filling in the correct pronoun. (You can look at the list in the 'Do you remember?' box if you need some help.)

a _____ is never too late to learn a new language.
b 'It gives _____ a whole new perspective,' _____ said.
c They speak Portuguese, when _____ don't want _____ to understand what _____ are saying!
d My brother lives in Iraq, but _____ doesn't speak any of the local languages.
e My family is trilingual; _____ speak three languages at home.

Demonstrative and indefinite pronouns

Demonstrative pronouns point out a specific person or thing. For example: this, that, these and those.

> Please listen to the podcast. Please listen to this.
>
> Remember this: if you can speak another language, it has great benefits.

Demonstrative pronouns also express contrast between

- people and things that are near – this, these
- people and things that are far away – that, those.

PRACTISE

1 Identify the demonstrative pronouns in these sentences.
   - a This is not the way we do things in our house.
   - b Put that away – you don't need it.
   - c The languages I wanted to learn are these: Spanish, Italian and French.
   - d Which of those do you want?

2 Now add the correct demonstrative pronoun to these sentences. Choose from:

this	that	these	those

   - a Take ______ to your grandmother; she's been looking for it.
   - b Being able to speak fluently – ______ is all I want!
   - c ______ is a story we tell in our family, about my grandfather.
   - d ______ are not good **translations**. Here, let me help you.

Indefinite pronouns refer to people in a general way. They are indefinite in number.

For example: some, one, anyone, someone, everyone, no one.

Everyone can speak their home language.

No one in my family can speak French.

PRACTISE

Identify the indefinite pronouns in these sentences.

1 She doesn't speak any other languages.
2 Anyone can speak their home language.
3 The one who looks like my mum speaks Spanish.
4 The other one does not speak English at all.

▲ When my grandfather came to America, his English was not very good. Listen to the anecdote about his visit to the doctor

CHALLENGE YOURSELF

Listen to Audio 1.3, a podcast about speaking another language.

- Explain to your partner why this story makes the family laugh.
- Draw a cartoon of the story, using speech bubbles for the words the young man says, and the doctor's words.
- Your cartoon should have only three frames, so choose which aspect of the story to represent in each frame.

Reading

English speakers abroad

Sometimes even English speakers don't understand each other!

- Have you spoken to English speakers from other countries?
- Did your English sound the same? What was similar?
- What was different? Think about your accents, different vocabulary or the way sentences are put together.

Read about a young actor's trip to Italy, with fellow English-speakers. As you read, think about these questions.

- What **version** of English do you speak?
- What are the special English words that you and your friends use?
- Are they different from the words you use in class?

Last year, I travelled with a team of actors around Italy, in a van, going from school to school, putting on plays in English. It was a very interesting experience – not just because we were English-speakers in a country where not everyone speaks English, but because we all spoke different versions of English too! I'm from England, Ava and Stella were from America, and Nick was from Australia. This led to some odd moments of **misunderstanding**. We didn't always understand one another!

'Ava, will you pass the biscuits please? They're in the glovebox.'

'The what? You mean the cookies?'

'Yes, please.'

'Where are they, did you say?'

'There – in the glovebox!'

'Oh you mean the glovie!' Nick said.

At which Nick and Stella started laughing, and Nick said, 'Watch out or you'll have a prang!'

'A what?' we asked.

'An accident, Pom!'

And so it went. Where I said flat, they said **apartment**. If I filled the van with petrol, they filled it with gas. I put our props in the boot and they opened the trunk to get our gear out. I went up in the lift and they came down in the elevator. The one who had the most fun was Nick, laughing all the time as he listened to us all trying to understand each other.

▲ Here's Nick putting our luggage in the boot. Or, as Ava would say, putting our bags in the trunk

▲ And this is me getting away from them all, with my book

Vocabulary and spelling

Read through the text again, carefully. Make a list of all the words that are British English, American English and Australian English. Create a table like this one in your notebook and add the words to the correct columns.

British English	American English	Australian English
biscuits	cookies	biscuits
		glovie

Can you think of any other examples of British, American and Australian English? Add them to your table.

Try this

Listen while your teacher plays a recording of a song called 'Let's call the whole thing off'. It comes from a movie called *Shall We Dance* (1937), and the song was written by Ira and George Gershwin.

Your teacher will give you a copy of the song lyrics.

1 Identify six indefinite and demonstrative pronouns in the first verse.
2 Make a list of all the words that have different pronunciations.
3 Which of the pronunciations is closest to the way you speak English in your community?
4 Choose five of the words in your list. Write down how you would say the words in your own English accent.

Present continuous tense

Do you remember?

The present continuous tense describes an action that continues in the present (now). It uses this form:

am/is/are + ing (form of the verb 'to be' + present participle). For example:

Which language are they speaking? They aren't speaking Italian, that I know!

We can also use the present continuous in the passive voice. It uses this form:

am/is/are + being + participle (form of the verb 'to be' + past participle). For example:

Before people only spoke one language in this country, but now other languages are being spoken too.

PRACTISE

Use the correct continuous forms of the verbs to complete these sentences.

1 He (is pack/is packing) his clothes because he (is be going/is going) on holiday tomorrow.
2 I do not understand the language they (is speaking/are speaking). Are they (speaking/speak) Mandarin Chinese perhaps?
3 She (is being taught/are be taught) Spanish by her Spanish grandmother.

Use of English

Second conditional

Discuss the answers to these questions with a partner.

1 How many languages do you speak?
2 What language do you speak at home?
3 Which languages are spoken in your community?
4 What language would you like to learn to speak? Explain why.

Now, working on your own, write down the answers to the questions above, in one paragraph.

▲ How many languages do you speak?

Do you remember?

Do you remember the wishful sentences you made in Lesson 2?

If I spoke ..., I would ...

Now you are going to learn more about how to express your wishes.

Second conditional clauses with 'if'

If clause	Second clause
If + simple past	Would + infinitive without 'to'
If this thing happened	Then this thing would happen too

We use the second conditional when we want to say the second thing will only happen if the first thing happens. For example:

If I spoke French, I would live in Paris and become an artist.

If I visited China, I would go to a noodle shop as soon as I got off the plane!

You can use the clauses in a different order too. For example:

I would live in Paris, if I spoke French.

PRACTISE

Complete these sentences with clauses starting with I / he / she / we / they / it would.

1 If I was fluent in Arabic, ...
2 If we spoke the same language, ...
3 If we were able to travel, ...
4 ..., if I was born in England.
5 If they moved to another country, ...
6 If she spoke three languages, ...
7 If I was bilingual, ...
8 If we were travel journalists, ...

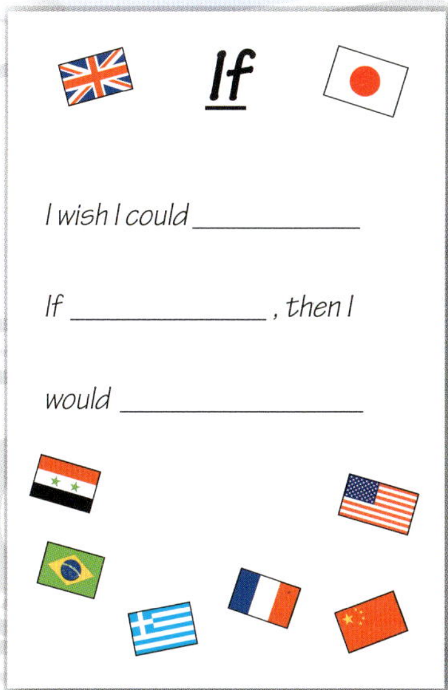

CHALLENGE YOURSELF

Make a wish list for your future. Use these forms, and make **at least** five wishes.
Write your wishes down. You could share them with a friend, if they are not too personal.

More pronouns

Quantitative pronouns indicate an indefinite quantity – some, any, none, one, much, many, little, few. For example:

You have so many books, may I borrow some?

You speak so many languages, will you teach me one?

Reciprocal pronouns are used to show that people are doing the same thing. We use 'each other' to refer to two people and 'one another' to refer to more than two people. For example:

Nick and Stella laughed at each other when they made mistakes.

The actors did not always understand one another because they spoke different forms of English.

PRACTISE

1 Make sentences with your partner. Offer your partner something. Let your partner accept or reject your offering, using the words some and any. Here are some examples.

Jamail: Would you like some of my lunch?

Shafika: No thanks, I don't want any.

Peter: Do you want some of my language books to practise?

Andrew: Yes please, I would like some.

2 Complete the paragraph by filling in the missing words. Use the words in the box, or your own choices.

one	many	none	any	some	much	few

I am going to travel next year. My parents offered me money, but I don't want ____________ from them, I just don't want to go with____________; I need just enough money to travel and speak different languages. I have learned a ____________. ____________ of them is Portuguese. ____________ say it is just like Spanish, but I don't agree. There are some words that are the same, but not ____________.

Reading

Travel tales

Have you ever made a mistake in another language? Most people who travel try and use the language of the country they are travelling in. Sometimes this can lead to very funny mistakes. Talk about this in your group.

- Have you ever made a mistake when speaking another language?
- How did the people you were talking to respond?
- Sometimes not understanding like this is called a 'language **barrier**'. Why do people use the word 'barrier'?

Read these stories about people making language mistakes, and the funny reactions they got from the local speakers of the language.

Travel tales

I'm a language teacher and I love travelling and blogging about my experiences. During my travels I often hear funny stories about language mistakes. This story I've heard many times as a language teacher. It has apparently happened in Indonesia, in Mexico and in Spain, so I suspect that it is an urban legend or urban myth. My favourite version is one with a man travelling in a taxi in Indonesia.

It is swelteringly hot, and the taxi has no air conditioning. The man gestures the driver to please open the window and says the word 'celana'. The driver looks horrified. 'Celana!' he insists. The driver now seems outraged. The man is trying to say the word 'celana', when asking to open the window. But 'celana' means pants; the word for window is 'gendala'. You can just picture the look on the driver's face ...!

Another funny story is the woman travelling in Paris, who was being followed by a stranger on the street. She turned around and shouted at the man: 'Léchez-moi!' He looked at her in horror and turned and left. When she told her family about it afterwards, they all started laughing. 'What's wrong?' she asked. Her children kindly explained that what she should have said was 'Laissez-moi!' – 'Leave me!' – not 'Léchez-moi!' which means 'Lick me!'

▲ A beautiful Parisian street

Returning to Indonesia, there was the expat who went to the hairdresser for the first time. She made the embarrassing mistake of confusing the word 'rambut' for hair, with 'ramput', meaning grass, and literally asked the hairdresser to just 'Trim off a bit of the grass'.

Vocabulary

Answer the questions.

1 Which of these is a good definition for an 'urban legend'?
  - a A story told about an urban area.
  - b A story that is handed down from person to person.
  - c A story that is not true, but is often repeated, so is believed by many to be true.

2 What does the man in Indonesia think he is saying, and what is he actually saying?

3 Why does the lady's family in Paris laugh at her?

4 What is the Indonesian word for 'hair'?

5 What is similar about all the stories?

6 The article uses different adjectives to describe how people responded to the language mishaps. Some of them are shown in the box below. Look up their meanings in your dictionary. Write down the meanings next to the word. Then make a sentence using that word. You can re-read the text to help you get a sense of the meanings of the words.

embarrassing	outraged	horrified

CHALLENGE YOURSELF

Create your own funny travel tale or 'language barrier' story that you could share with your class.

Speaking and listening

Benefits of language learning

1 Listen to Audio 1.4 about these five fantastic reasons to learn a new language. As you listen, tick off the five reasons on this list. Then put the reasons in the correct order in which they were mentioned.

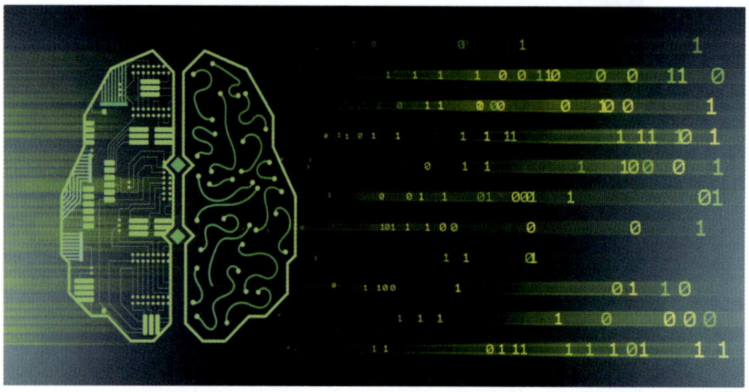

◀ Learning another language actually makes your brain tissue denser (and that's a good thing)!

Improves memory	Boast to your friends
Connect directly	Sharpens the mind
Build a bigger brain	Gain perspective
Improves the first language	Broaden your mind
Live longer and **prosper**	Advance your career
Get a better job	Deepen your connection

2 Talk about these questions in pairs.

a Why does bilingual brain tissue become denser?

b What kind of diseases does this denser brain tissue delay?

c What does the phrase 'connect directly' mean? Choose from this list.

- Connect on the phone.
- Speak to people in their own language.
- Direct people to the **connection**.

d Why do employers want bilingual employees?

e How does learning another language 'broaden your mind'?

LET'S TALK

In your group, discuss the list of great reasons to learn a new language.

- Do you agree on the top five reasons?
- Which other reasons on the list do you think are important, and why?
- Which reasons mean the same thing? Cross them off the list.
- Can your group agree on the top three benefits of bilingual learning? Write these down in your notebook.

Writing

Posting a challenge!

▶ Here's an example of a language poster. Do you think it's a good poster? Say why or why not

CHALLENGE YOURSELF

You are going to make a poster about the benefits of learning a second language. Think about the questions below.

Planning

- What message do I want to communicate? Decide on one main idea. You can use one of the ideas from the first exercise, or your own idea.
- What words and picture will communicate my message well?
- What colours should I use?
- Where do I want to put the words and the picture?
- Can I use some of the new language I have learned in this unit?

Drafting

- Design a rough draft of your poster in your notebook.
- Show where the words and picture will be.

Revision

Read your draft carefully. Think of ways you can improve it, before you make a neat copy on poster paper. Ask yourself:

- Is the picture clear and big enough?
- Is my message coming through?
- Are the words bold enough?
- Do the colours suit my message?

Editing and presenting

- Edit your ideas and ask a friend to check your language for errors.
- Make a neat copy on your poster paper and display your poster in class.

Write a narrative essay

Try this

- What are these bilingual signs saying?
- Do you know the two languages on each sign?
- How does the picture help you with the meaning?
- Would you have understood the signs without the pictures?
- Write the message on each sign in your home language.

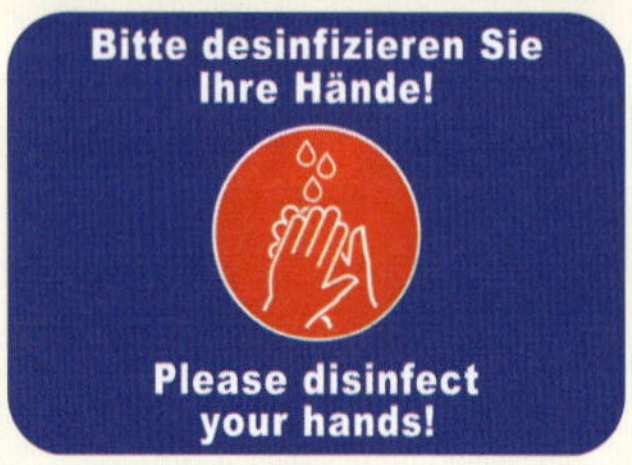

1 You are going to write your short narrative essay about something funny that happened, which involved a language miscommunication. Talk about your ideas with your partner. Start by making a mind map of your ideas. Use this outline to help you.

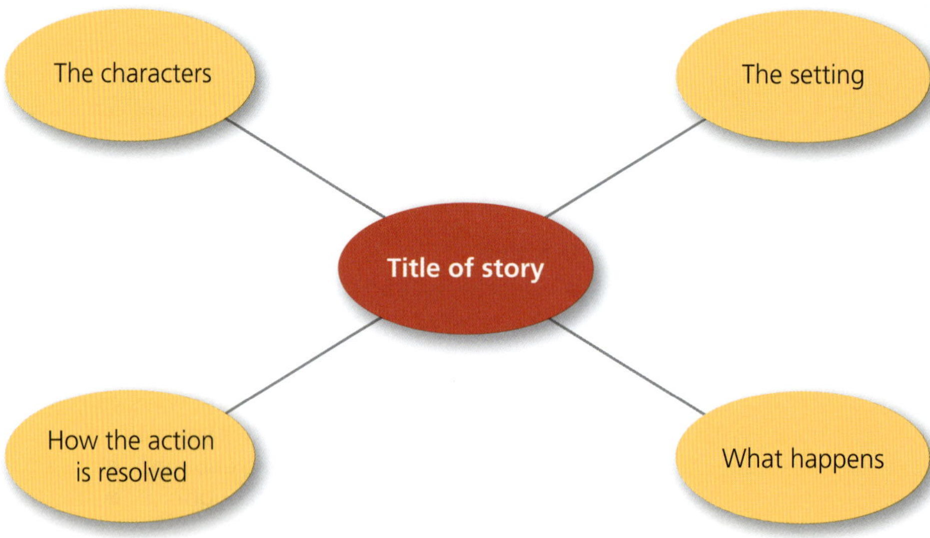

2 Now write your essay in your notebook.
- You should have at least three paragraphs – one to introduce the idea, another for the action or event, and a final paragraph to resolve what happened.
- Follow the same revision and editing process as you did with your poster.
- When you have made corrections, write out a neat copy to hand in to your teacher.

Self check

- Make sure you have three paragraphs. Each paragraph should have one main topic sentence and two or three supporting sentences.
- Use demonstrative and indefinite pronouns in your essay.
- Use the second conditional to help make the story funny, for example: If only I spoke _______ this would not have happened!

What can you do?

Read and review what you can do.
- I can listen to a radio interview, a song and a podcast about speaking English.
- I can talk about being bilingual and about speaking different languages.
- I can read infographics about English, a personal anecdote about language, and stories about language mix-ups.
- I can write a narrative essay and design a poster.
- I can use pronouns, the second conditional, and various question forms to discuss language.

Now you have completed Unit 1, you may like to try the Unit 1 online knowledge test if you are using the Boost eBook.

2 Room to live

In this unit you will:

- listen to texts about living **spaces**
- listen to an argument about building homes cheaply and quickly
- talk about spaces in which we live and compare them
- read about how to **declutter** your own spaces
- read about homes in the future
- use verbs in the active and passive voice to express the present and the future
- use adverbs to make comparisons and use prepositions before nouns and adjectives
- complete a group project about designing a living space
- write a report on the group project.

▲ Homes in an old town

▲ Different types of homes in a big city

▲ A house with a garden in a suburb

▲ A tent in the desert

Speaking and listening

Living spaces

▲ A small mobile home

We all have different spaces where we live. Some of us live in houses, others live in apartments. Some houses and apartments are big, others are small. Some of us live in cities or towns, and others live in the countryside.

Work in groups. Describe your home living space to your group. Try to do this in one sentence. For example:

I live with my family in an old house with two bedrooms in the middle of a town.

Look at the pictures and read the captions. Then listen to Audio 2.1, a short talk about living spaces. Read the definitions of words in the HINT box and make sure you understand these words.

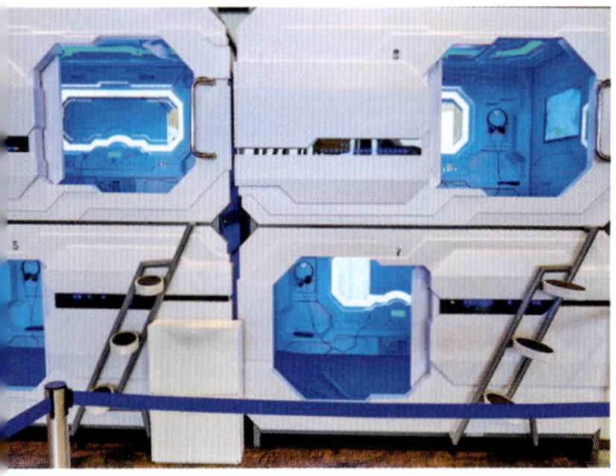

▲ Sleeping pods in a hotel

HINT

Permanent means to continue to do something for a long time.

Mobile means to move around. A tent is a type of **mobile** home.

A *pod* is a small container that **fits** around something. The seeds of plants are often inside pods.

Try this

Listen to Audio 2.1 about living spaces again. Choose four of the sentences below to summarise the text you listened to.

1 People who live in cities usually have smaller living spaces.
2 People who live outside cities may have bigger living spaces.
3 All the people who live in cities live in apartments.
4 In the future, our living spaces will be different.
5 In the future, we will all sleep in pods and tents.
6 We will have more personal **possessions** in the future.

PRACTISE

1 Listen to Audio 2.1 again and practise saying these words with the correct word stress.

living spaces future permanent mobile available personal possessions probably

2 Work in pairs. Listen and then discuss how the intonation is different in the statement, question and exclamation.

- People who live in big cities usually have small living spaces.
- What will our living spaces look like in the future?
- If that happens, we are all going to have to be very neat and tidy!

Speaking and listening

Listen to the story *A space to read*

1 Before you listen to the story, look at the picture and ask yourself these questions:

- Who is the main **character** in this story?
- What does he enjoy doing?
- Where does he live?

2 Now listen to Audio 2.2, *A space to read*.

Try this

Now work in pairs. Listen to Audio 2.2 again and summarise the main ideas of the story. Use words and phrases from the box.

apartment	family	read	shares	tenth
he has no space for this	space for himself	makes a shelf		
folds his clothes and puts them away	makes up his bed			

You can start like this:

A space to read

Jonas lives in an _______________ on the _______________ floor.

He lives with his _______________ and _______________ a room with his brothers.

He likes to _______________ but _______________.

So he decides to make a _______________.

First, he _______________.

Then, he _______________.

He made _______________.

Share your ideas with the rest of the class.

PRACTISE

1 Read what some other students said about their own rooms.

I am so lucky! I have a big bedroom with lots of space.

I share a bedroom with my sister who is very neat!

I have such a small room but at least I have my own space.

I work, eat and sleep happily in my bedroom.

My room feels bigger than it really is because I have places to put all my things.

2 Work in groups. Describe your living spaces or bedrooms at home and compare them with others.

- Does your space look like either of the pictures below?
- Describe your space or room to your group.
- Say what you think about your space.

CHALLENGE YOURSELF

Draw a picture of your space or bedroom at home and write two or three sentences to describe the space.

Use of English

Adverbs

Do you remember?

Adverbs tell you more about verbs. You can use adverbs to compare actions. To do this we use comparative and superlative forms of adverbs.

Work in pairs. Can you identify the adverbs in these sentences? Some of them are adverbs that Jonas and his brothers used in the story you listened to.

1 'Can't you play more quietly?' Jonas asked impatiently.
2 'I am busy and I am working hard.'
3 'We're working harder than you are,' laughed Mike.
4 My room feels bigger than it really is.
5 She spoke the most carefully when she described her living space.
6 You draw the most beautifully in our group. Can you draw your room to show us?

PRACTISE

How do you form comparative and superlative adverbs?

Explain what you would do with the adverbs to complete the sentences below.

1 Jonas works (quiet). He works (quiet) than his brothers.
2 The boys play (noisy).
3 He started to speak (slow). He spoke the (slow) of everyone in the group.

We can use adverbs to make the meaning of another adverb or adjective stronger.

Study the underlined adverbs in these sentences which describe someone's living space.

> My living space – Lesley
>
> I wish I had a bit more space for myself. My bedroom is quite a lot smaller than yours. I don't like sharing it with my sister very much either! I think I need slightly more space than she does because I have more books and clothes. But my bedroom is still the part of the house that I like the most. The kitchen is the space I enjoy the least!

PRACTISE

Choose the best words to complete each sentence and write the sentences in your notebook.

1 Our house is (a bit bigger/a bigger bit) than my cousin's house.
2 There is (slight less/**slightly** less) space in this apartment.
3 I like sharing a bedroom (very much/very more)! It's fun.
4 There is (**quite** a lot/a lot quite) of space on the shelf that you could use for your possessions.
5 'Could you make (a bit less noise/a noise less bit) please?' asked Paul. 'I'm trying to work.'

Try this

Work in pairs. Describe your home or your bedroom to your partner. Use as many of these phrases as you can in your description.

much more	slightly more	slightly less	the most
a bit more	a bit less	quite a lot	the least

Verbs in the present tense

HINT

Think about the verbs that you use to give instructions (the imperative).

Do you remember?

1 Which verb tense did you use to give a description of your home at the beginning of the unit?

Here are some examples of what some other students said.

I live with my grandparents in an apartment in a big town.

We live in a large house with three bedrooms and a garden.

My home is **shared** by my family and my cousins.

Our house is enormous. It is far too big for us!

2 Some sentences are in the active voice and one is in the passive voice. Can you identify these?

3 Why do we we use the passive voice?

PRACTISE

Write these sentences correctly in your notebook.

1 She (lives/live) in a big house with her family and her cousins.

2 We (have/has) quite a big apartment in the middle of town.

3 The apartment (is/are) shared by two families.

4 The brothers (run/runs) around noisily in the bedroom.

5 Jonas (decides/decide) to make a space for himself in his bedroom.

6 All his possessions (is packing/are packed) away neatly on a shelf now.

Try this

Work in pairs. Read the description of the room below to your partner. Choose the correct verbs as you do this.

This (is/was) a very untidy room. The person who (uses/using) this space is quite messy. There (are/be) things all over the floor. Can you (seen/see) the clothes on the floor? I can (be seeing/see) cups on the desk and on the printer too! Where does the person (sit/sat)? There (is/are) things everywhere! Maybe this room (is used/is using) by many people.

Reading

Read a text with instructions

Does your living space look anything like the rooms in the pictures below? Maybe you need some advice about how to declutter your living space?

1 Before you read, discuss what you think 'to declutter' means.
2 Read the following text. Read the headings first. They will give you an idea about what you will read. Then read the paragraphs under each heading.

HINT
The prefix de- means 'to take or move away' or 'the opposite'.

Other words with this prefix are deforest, decrease, decaffeinate.

How to declutter your living space

Decluttering is not that difficult. Just follow these easy tips.

TIP 1 Clear out and clean
The first thing you need to do is to take everything out. Open your cupboards and drawers. Look on top of the shelves. Lift up the carpets. Move the lamps. If you can, take everything to another room. Then, when the room is clear, look at the furniture. Do you need it all? If you don't, take it out too. Then, clean everything and repair broken things. After that, rearrange the furniture to create as much space as you can. We all need space to move around.

TIP 2 Sort everything into piles
Sort out your things into **piles**. If you are decluttering a bedroom, make sure clothes are put in one pile and books in another pile, for example.

TIP 3 Get rid of things you don't use
The next step is a big one. Now you have to choose and you have to be quite determined as well. Ask yourself: What do I really need? What don't I need? Then, put the things you don't need in one pile. You can throw things away or **donate** them to someone else.

TIP 4 Repack everything neatly
This is a fun part. Now you have a clear room and you can pack away things that you really need and like. Arrange everything neatly. You do not have to fill every space in the room. Leave some space open.

Try this

Work in small groups. Take turns to ask and answer questions about the text you have read. Try to ask different questions. Make sure you know the answers to the questions you ask. For example:

- What is the first thing you must do to declutter a room?
- Must you throw away everything you don't want?
- What does the word 'pile' mean?

Vocabulary and spelling

1 Write down the names of four items of furniture mentioned in the text 'How to declutter you living space'. Make sure you know how to spell these words.

2 Here are some expressions from the text. Choose the correct preposition.

a I need to clear (out/of) my bedroom. It's a mess.

b He has far too many clothes. He needs to get rid (of/out) some.

c What should I throw (away/in) and what should I keep?

d Mara first sorted (out/away) her possessions into piles.

3 Work in pairs. Use each of the expressions in sentences of your own.

HINT

The best tips are often the simplest things. People will remember them and try them out!

LET'S TALK

Work in groups. Talk about the tips that you read.

- Can you think of anything else that you can do to declutter a room? Each group should think of another three good tips. Make some notes as you talk.
- Then, share your new tips with the class.
- Have a class vote. Which are the five best tips for decluttering?

CHALLENGE YOURSELF

Make a small poster with your five best tips for decluttering.

Write the tips as headings. For example:

DECLUTTER YOUR ROOM

Tip 1 - Put everything into piles.

Tip 2 -

You can do this on a laptop or tablet. Try out different layouts and different sizes of print to make your poster look interesting.

Use of English

Prepositions with nouns and adjectives

Do you remember?

A phrase is a group of words without a verb. We often use prepositions to start these phrases and we call these prepositional phrases. Work in pairs.

1 Can you find the phrases that start with prepositions in the sentences below?

2 Can you identify an adjective and a noun in each phrase?

a He shares a small bedroom with two younger brothers.

b Our apartment is on the second floor.

c In the future, we may sleep in small sleeping pods.

d Take everything to another room.

e He fills every space in the room with books and games.

f Jonas put all his personal possessions on the top shelf.

PRACTISE

Give the person who uses this room some advice about decluttering. Complete these sentences with prepositional phrases. Choose from the prepositions in the box to start your phrases. You don't have to use all the prepositions in the box.

in	on	over	under	into

1 Pick up all the papers ...

2 Put all the pens and pencils ...

3 Put your dirty clothes ...

4 Arrange the books ...

CHALLENGE YOURSELF

Make these descriptions more interesting by adding adjectives in the prepositional phrases.

1 One day, I hope to live in a house.

2 We live in an apartment.

3 I put all my shoes in the cupboard.

4 We stayed in a hotel while we were on holiday.

Future passive

Do you remember?

We can express the future in different ways in the active voice:

- *going to* + verb stem: to describe plans and arrangements that have already been made
- *will* + verb stem: to make predictions
- the present tense: to describe future arrangements with fixed dates.

Can you identify the future forms in these examples?

- We are going to share a room in the hotel.
- There will be less space in the cities, so we will all have smaller living spaces.
- Building on the new houses begins in April.

PRACTISE

Work in pairs. Use the given words to make sentences and questions about the future.

1. What I (to do) with all of these possessions?
2. Where you (to live) next year?
3. This (to be) a beautiful living space when it is complete.
4. I (to declutter) my room on Saturday evening.
5. From next week, I (to share) a room with my brother.

We can also express the future in the passive voice. For example:

All the rooms in the new hotel will be equipped with sleeping pods.

We will be forced to share our living spaces.

We form the future passive with will + be + the past participle.

Try this

Write these sentences in the future passive form, using the given verbs.

1. Our homes (to adapt) in the future.
2. Technology (to use) to make homes more comfortable.
3. More homes (to build) entirely by machines.
4. Everyone (to ask) to share their living spaces with more people.
5. Goods (to move) from one place to another by drones.
6. All unnecessary clutter (to clear) away.

HINT

Remember that some verbs have irregular past participles. Look at the list of irregular participles on pages 161–62.

Reading

Predicting future living spaces

▲ The future? A house flown by a drone

What do you think our living spaces will be like in the future? Before you read this article, discuss these questions with a partner. You can also make a few quick sketches of what a home could look like in the future. Think about:

- How will homes be built?
- What type of technology will be used?
- Will we use artificial intelligence (AI), robots and drones?

Read the magazine article. Make a note of any words that you do not understand. Then, when you reread the article, try to work out the meanings from the context. You can use a dictionary as well.

HOMES OF THE FUTURE

People believe that there will be big changes to our homes and our personal spaces in the future. Towns, cities and living spaces will have to be built to fit more people. Living spaces will need to be adapted for different purposes. And there are lots of ideas around about what these new living spaces will look like. You only need to watch the movies to get an idea of what some of these amazing, imaginary places will be like.

One idea is that we will live in houses which will change shape and size according to who is in the house at the time. The walls and floors of a house will be made of a material that can change shape quickly, a bit like our skin!

Another idea is that everything inside the house will be controlled **remotely**. Well, this is fast becoming a reality as some people can already do this! So we will have apps on our phones and we will use the apps to cook supper, record shows, let the cat in and out, and so on.

And then there is the decoration of the living space. Maybe we will be able to change the colour and shape of things as we get bored with what we have. Say you have a brown sofa with green cushions. After a few months, you decide you would prefer a pink sofa with purple cushions! And so you change the colours! Just like that! Every home would have a three-dimensional (3D) printer to make new furniture at the touch of a button. Fun maybe, but what will happen to all the furniture we do not want?

On a more serious note, all the power needed by a **household** will be generated by the house, probably using solar energy. Each household will also be adapted to get rid of all the waste that it generates too. No more rubbish dumps!

And what about if you wanted to move to a different place? They say we will be able to get a drone to move the whole house. So we won't have to move all our things from one house to another.

Perhaps in a hundred years from now, or even sooner, our living spaces will be like living organisms that adapt to all of our needs.

Vocabulary

1 Choose the word in the box that matches each definition.

drone	imaginary	remotely	reality	generate

a from a distance

b to make

c the way something really is

d something that you picture in your mind

e a computer-controlled machine that can fly around and do different things

Answer the questions.

2 What are two possible ways in which living spaces will change in the future?

3 Where can you see good examples of imaginary houses of the future?

4 Name two things that apps on our phones can or will be able to control in our living spaces.

5 Name one way in which drones will perhaps be useful.

Read the article again and then complete the sentences in your notebook.

6 In the future, living spaces will need to be adapted because ___________.

a there will be fewer people on Earth
b there will be more people on Earth
c we will not be able to use solar power

7 The idea that we can use apps to control things inside our homes ___________.

a is already possible
b is not possible
c may be possible in the future

8 If something works 'at the touch of a button', ___________.

a it needs solar energy to work
b it is quick and easy to work, like touching a button
c it is difficult to work, like switching a button on and off

9 You may be able to use ___________ to make new furniture for your home in the future.

a an AI printer
b solar energy
c a 3D printer

Try this

Discuss this question as a class.

The author expresses opinions in this article about changes to our living spaces. Which of the following does the author believe will be good?

- Homes will be able to change shape and size.
- Living spaces will make their own power.
- Living spaces will get rid of their own waste.
- People will change their furniture all the time.

Speaking and listening

Listen to an explanation

Look at the diagram below and read the labels carefully. It shows how a 3D printer may be used in the future to build a house more quickly and cheaply than we can do at present. Then listen to Audio 2.3 which is an explanation of how 3D printing works.

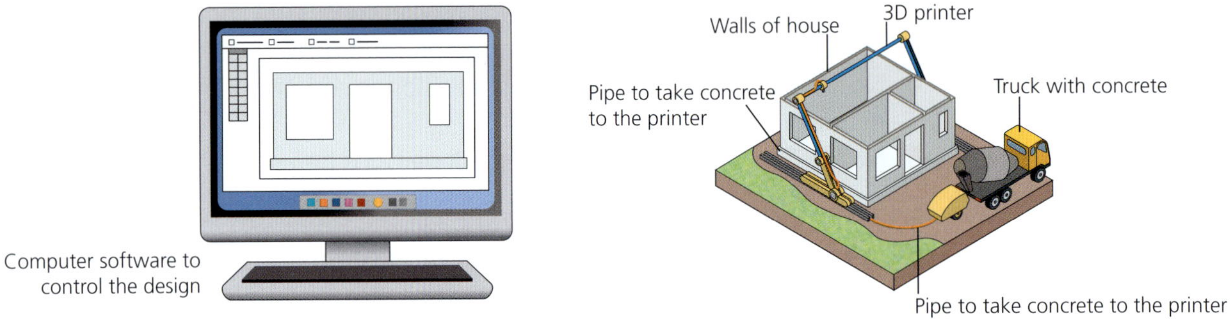

▲ A house made by 3D printing

PRACTISE

Listen to the text about 3D printing again. Say if these statements are true or false.

1 A 3D printer can make the walls and floors of a house.
2 To make a 3D home, you need glue, nails and a computer.
3 3D printers build walls in layers, using a mixture called **concrete**.
4 3D homes will be quicker and easier to build than homes made of bricks or wood.
5 A 3D printer can easily be moved from one place to another to build homes.
6 A 3D **laser** printer builds all the parts of a house.
7 3D printers are controlled by robots, so no people are involved in the building process.
8 The only way we can build cheap houses in the future is by 3D printing.

Try this

1 Draw and label a diagram to explain the concept of laser printing a house. You can do this by hand or on a computer.
2 Share your drawing with a partner and explain the idea using your drawing. Use some of these words and phrases in your explanation:

doors walls windows concrete layers mobile 3D printer You need this to ... The printer puts down ... On the spot ...

LET'S TALK

The explanation that you listened to makes an argument. It says that 3D printing is the best way to build houses in the future.

The following reasons are given to support this argument.

- 3D printing is quicker than **traditional** building.
- 3D printing is cheaper than traditional building.
- You only need a few things to print a house.
- 3D printers are mobile.

But what does the argument not say? Are there things in the argument that are not completely true? Is there another side to this argument? Let's analyse and evaluate the argument.

STEP 1: Work in groups and discuss the argument. Try to evaluate it. Use these questions:

- Who do you think wrote the argument about 3D printers? (What is the source of the information?)
- Could there be a reason for making this argument?
- How can you check the information in the article?

STEP 2: Then analyse the argument. Use these questions:

- Will people such as builders lose their jobs because of this new technology?
- What is the cost of the 3D printers? Could everyone afford to buy or hire one to use?
- Do the 3D printers cause any ecological damage? Will there be consequences for our living areas?

STEP 3: Then look at these images of communities working to build cheap homes quickly for their own communities. Discuss what they are doing.

- What materials are they using?
- How are they helping each other?

STEP 4: Have a short class debate about the best way to build cheap houses quickly in the future.

HINT

Make some notes during your discussion. You may be able to use these notes in the project that you will complete later in the unit.

▲ People putting up the frame of a house, working together

▲ People in an African village building a traditional home together with natural materials

CHALLENGE YOURSELF

In your groups, present a short argument to the class about another way of building homes quickly and cheaply.

Illustrate your talk with pictures or diagrams if possible.

Do you remember?

The correct punctuation makes a text easy to read and understand. For example:

- Full stops, commas and colons show the reader when to pause.
- Capital letters give names or abbreviations.
- Question marks and exclamation marks alert us to different types of sentences.
- Speech marks are used for quotations or to emphasise words.

Writing

Punctuation in reports

PRACTISE

Rewrite this section of a report with punctuation that will make it easier to read.

> **three dimensional printed houses**
>
> in the future we will build homes quickly and cheaply using a **three-dimensional** 3d laser technology to print homes a 3 d printer builds a solid object by adding material in layers
>
> In traditional building different parts of the building are made in factories then they are fitted together using special tools other components are used to put the pieces together for example cement concrete glue nails metal rods

Project

You are going to work in groups to design your ideal living space for the future. Then, you will write a report about the project. Would your living space be something like a space station on the Moon? Or would you try to bring plants into your home? There are many options.

Here are some steps you can follow to prepare for your report.

Try this

STEP 1: A group discussion

- Have a group discussion about your ideal living space in the future. What might be needed in the future?
- Think about the ideas covered in this unit and look at your notes.
- Prepare some new ideas to add to the discussion. Do a search on the internet for future living spaces and see if you can find any interesting ideas.
- Create a mind map with your ideas.

STEP 2: Agree on the living space you want to design

- Write down three or four main features of your living area.
- Work in pairs and draw some rough designs.
- Discuss your designs as a group.
- Make neat diagrams of the designs that you like the best as a group. Label the designs to show the key ideas.

STEP 3: Draft a report which you can present to the class. Your report should be about 250 words long and you can do this by hand or on a computer. You should use headings and at least one diagram in the report. Your diagram can be a sketch of the living space or it can show how you will build the living space. You can use the present or the future tenses, as necessary.

HINT

- Think about the space the living area will take. How many people will live there and how will they share the space?
- Think about ecology. What materials will be used? Will they cause any damage to the environment?
- Headings will help you to structure your report. Start with the headings. We do not use full stops in headings. For example:
  Our ideal living space **Our plan**

Self check

- Add prepositional phrases to make the content of your report interesting. For example: in the main sleeping area, around the expanding walls.
- Compare your ideal design to other designs using adverbs.
- Use *will* to make predictions about the future.
- Use *going to* to describe what you plan to do.
- Check your punctuation carefully.

What can you do?

Read and review what you can do.

- I can understand arguments about building homes cheaply and quickly.
- I can talk about and describe living spaces.
- I can read explanations about living spaces.
- I can use verbs in the active and passive voice to express the present and the future.
- I can use adverbs to make comparisons and use prepositions before nouns and adjectives.
- I can contribute to a group project about designing a living space.

Now you have completed Unit 2, you may like to try the Unit 2 online knowledge test if you are using the Boost eBook.

3 Storytelling

In this unit you will:
- listen to traditional tales and a film review
- talk about modern tales, traditional tales and the tradition of storytelling
- read traditional stories and fairy tales
- write your own story from a different point of view
- use past tenses, adjectives, connectives and the active and passive voice.

Speaking and listening

Whose story is it?

1 Work in a group of four. Look at the pictures on the opposite page.
   a Do you know which traditional story each picture represents?
   b Talk about the names of the stories, as you know them.
   c Choose one and tell the story as you know it to the rest of your group.

Every fairy story is about a group of characters. They can be people or animals. They are all in a certain place, which writers call the **setting**. Something happens, or there is action of some kind. This is called the **plot**. Then there is the ending, which sometimes tells you the **moral** of the story.

2 Look at the diagram representing the structure of the story. Now choose one of the pictures on the opposite page. Talk about the story represented by this picture.
   a Who are the characters?
   b Describe the setting.
   c What happens (the plot)?
   d How does the story end?

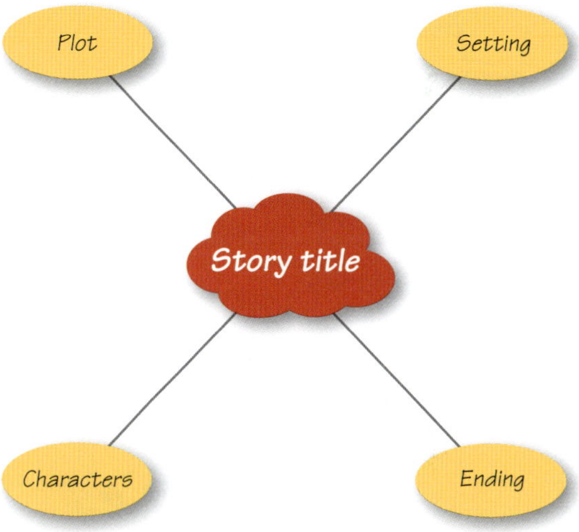

▲ 'The Fox and the Crow'

3 Listen to Audio 3.1, the story of 'The Fox and the **Crow**'. As you listen, try and identify
- the characters
- the setting, or where the story takes place
- the plot
- the ending
- the moral of the story.

HINT
The **moral** of the story is what the reader learns or the message of the story. Many animal fables, like 'The Fox and the Crow', are meant to teach the reader something.

PRACTISE
The fox flatters the crow, using many descriptive words. Fill in the missing words. Use words from the box to help you.

graceful	beautiful	mightier	sweetly

'Good afternoon, Miss Crow,' said Fox. 'How ________ you look today. Your feathers shine in the light. Your neck is as ________ as a swan's, and your wings ________ than an eagle's. I am sure that if you had a voice, you would sing as ________ as a **nightingale**.'

Speaking and listening

Listen to a fairy tale

1 Talk about stories that everyone in the class knows. Do you know any of these stories? Tell them to the class.

Start like this:	Who were in this place …
Once upon a time …	Then this happened …
There were these characters …	At the end, …

Hansel and Gretel	*Ali Baba and the 40 Thieves*
Goldilocks and the Three Bears	*Why the Sea is Salty*
Why Anansi has Eight Thin Legs	*The Dragon Princess*
Papa Bois	*Sang Kancil*
How the Tiger Got its Stripes	*Why Mosquitoes Buzz in Your Ear*

▲ Ali Baba

2 Discuss these questions with a partner.
- a What is your favourite fairy tale?
- b Who is your favourite fairy tale character? Why do you say so?
- c How does the fairy tale end?
- d Does it have a moral?

3 Listen to the story of 'Little Red Riding Hood' in Audio 3.2. In your group, discuss these questions about the story.
- a Who are the 'good guys' and who is the 'bad guy' in this story?
- b What does the Wolf think when he sees Red Riding Hood?
- c What three observations does Red Riding Hood make when she is feeling uncertain about whether she is really speaking to her grandmother?
- d Does this story have a moral? If it does, what would you say the moral is?

◀ *Goldilocks and the Three Bears*

Describing people and events

Do you remember?

You know that adjectives tell you more about nouns.

For example:

He is a good storyteller.

She put on her red coat.

PRACTISE

This story is full of interesting adjectives which add to the atmosphere of the tale.

Find the adjectives in these sentences. Write them in your notebook.

1 Red Riding Hood put on her red cloak.
2 'There's a mouth-watering meal,' the Wolf said.
3 He spoke in a wobbly Granny voice.
4 'What big ears you have,' she said.
5 She had a worried look on her face.
6 A passing woodcutter heard her screams.
7 This tale has a good ending.
8 They sat down to enjoy a well-deserved cup of tea.

CHALLENGE YOURSELF

Work in groups of four. Act out the story of Little Red Riding Hood, following these steps:

- Each of you takes one part – Red Riding Hood, Grandmother, the Wolf and the woodcutter.
- Use the adjectives from the Practise activity when you plan what you are going to say. For example, mouth-watering, red, wobbly, etc. Add exciting adjectives of your own.
- Present your short play to the rest of the class.

Try this

Complete this dialogue with a partner.

RRH: What big ears you have, my dear!

Granny: ...

RRH: What big eyes you have, my dear!

Granny: ...

RRH: What big teeth you have, my dear!

Granny: ...

▲ What big big teeth you have, my dear!

Use of English

Adjectives

Adjectives add colour and interest to a story, so they are very important in storytelling.

Do you remember?

Here's a quick activity for you to revise what you already know about degrees of comparison and adjectives.

1 Copy this table into your notebook and fill in the missing words.

good		best
bad	worse	
	faster	fastest
strong		
	happier	
	more intelligent	the most intelligent
beautiful	more beautiful	

2 Now make sentences with each set of adjectives in the table and write them in your notebook. For example:

I think I am bad, but the Wolf is worse than me, and the woodcutter is the worst of all; he chopped off the Wolf's head!

HINT

If the adjective has more than three syllables you use 'more' or 'most' when you compare things. For example: '**talented**' has three syllables – ta-len-ted, so we say:

He is more talented, and she is the most talented.

Compound adjectives are formed when two descriptive words are joined together by a hyphen. Often, participles make up the second half of the compound adjective.

For example:

She would make a mouth-watering snack. (watering is a present participle)

Aladdin and His Lamp is a well-known fairy tale. (known is a past participle)

Try this

Choose the correct compound adjective to complete each sentence below.

brightly-lit old-fashioned short-lived good-looking quick-thinking warm-hearted well-behaved time-saving ready-made

1 I like listening to ________________ fairy tales; I'm not fond of the modern versions.
2 Cinderella went to the ball, where she danced with a ________________ prince.
3 The ________________ ballroom sparkled with a million candles.
4 She was a ________________ girl, even though her step-sisters had treated her unkindly.
5 Grandmother had some ________________ cakes for tea.
6 The ________________ woodcutter saved Red Riding Hood's life.

Making connections in stories

1 Work with a partner. First, use as many adjectives as you can, of any type, to describe this setting. You can use compound adjectives, or comparisons.

2 Next, think of three actions that could happen in this setting. Use this frame to help you.
First, … Then, … Finally, …
Discuss your ideas with your partner. Then write them down.
3 Share your three actions with the class. Who had the most interesting three-line story to tell?

CHALLENGE YOURSELF

Do some research on an ancient Greek writer named Aesop, who lived more than 2500 years ago. You will find him in any encyclopaedia or by searching online. He wrote stories like 'The Fox and the Crow' and 'The Fox and the Grapes'.

- Find out five interesting facts about Aesop.
- Write them down and be prepared to talk to the class about them in the next lesson.

Try this

1 First, listen to the story of 'The Fox and the Grapes' in Audio 3.3.
2 Then, work with a partner to put the following sentences in order, to tell the story you have just heard. Pay attention to connecting words like first, then, finally, again.

▲ Could this be where the expression 'sour grapes' comes from?

a First, he jumped to try and reach the grapes.
b Fox was starving as he had not eaten breakfast or lunch.
c Again, he missed.
d Fox said, 'I wasn't really very hungry'.
e He walked past a vineyard.
f A big, juicy bunch of grapes was dangling just over the wall.
g Then he took a few steps back, ran and jumped again.
h He missed.
i Finally, Fox decided the grapes were probably sour.

Reading

Read a modern fairy tale

1 What is a modern fairy tale? Discuss this in your group.

a Are the *Harry Potter* books a modern fairy tale? What about the *His Dark Materials* trilogy? Or the *Twilight* series of books?

b Give some examples of **fantasy** stories and fairy tales you know.

2 Read this modern version of 'Little Red Riding Hood'. As you read, consider these questions.

a How do the characters, plot and setting differ from the traditional version of the story?

b How does the moral of the story differ from the traditional version?

Red's Revenge

Red was bored. She decided to visit her Gran. She pulled on her red hoodie and stuck her mobile phone into her pocket.

'Ma, I'm going over to Gran's house,' she shouted.

'Remember what I told you about not talking to strangers,' her mother said.

'Yes, yes, you've told me a hundred times,' mumbled Red as she put in her earphones and put her playlist onto shuffle.

The Wolf saw her from behind a bus stop as she walked down the road. 'In-te-res-ting,' he said to himself. He started to follow her.

But Red wasn't stupid. She saw him out of the corner of her eye. And she knew her folktales. She got cross. Red-hot angry! (She wasn't called Red for nothing.)

'Time to turn this around,' she said to herself, as she flagged down a taxi and jumped in. The Wolf caught the next taxi as Red pulled out her phone and dialled a number.

Mr Security from the **guard** company was waiting for her when she arrived at her Gran's. Quick as a wink, they put their plan into action. Red and Gran hid in the cupboard, and Mr Security put on Gran's clothes and climbed into her bed.

There was a knock at the door.

'Come in dearie,' said Mr Security, in a wobbly Granny voice.

'Granny, what big eyes you have,' said the Wolf, looking a bit uncertain.

'All the better to see you with, my dear,' said Mr Security.

'And Granny, what big ears you have,' said the Wolf, who had the feeling his day was about to go horribly wrong.

'All the better to hear you with, my dear.'

'And Granny, what big … MUSCLES you have!' said the Wolf with a scream as he bolted for the door. But the back-up team were waiting for him, and with one swoop, they tied him up and threw him in the van.

Red and Gran got out of the cupboard and sat down with the Mr Security to enjoy a well-deserved cup of tea, with fresh cakes.

And they all lived happily ever after.

3 Answer these questions in your notebook.
  a Who are the characters in the story?
  b Why does Red mumble, 'Yes, yes' when her mother speaks to her?
  c Why do you think the Wolf says, 'In-te-res-ting'? Why do you think he spoke like this? What do you think he was thinking of? Do you think he might have plans to do something to Red?
  d What does Red mean when she says 'Time to turn this around'?
  e What is the main difference between this story and the traditional version?
  f What is the moral of the story, in your opinion?
  g Which version of the story do you prefer? Give a reason for your answer.

Vocabulary and spelling

1 Change the meaning of the sentences by replacing the underlined words with words of opposite meaning. Write the new sentences in your notebook.
  a Red was icy calm.
  b The wicked Wolf caught the soft-hearted girl.
  c It was a dark and stormy night.
  d The old man married the well-dressed woman.

2 Many expressions in English use colour. These are just a few of the expressions that include the colour red. There are many expressions that use other colours as well. Make sentences with these expressions to show that you know what they mean. You can use a dictionary to help you.

red-faced seeing red caught red-handed a red herring
the red carpet a red-letter day

3 Learn to spell these words. Start with the first part of each word, which is short and easy. Note that the second part is always a participle. Make sure you put the hyphen between the two parts of the word.

mouth-watering old-fashioned well-deserved good-looking
quick-thinking warm-hearted well-behaved time-saving ready-made

CHALLENGE YOURSELF

How many other English expressions can you think of that have to do with colour? Complete these phrases, and then use them in sentences of your own. Add your own examples too.

as ________ as a sheet ________ with rage
as ________ as grass as ________ as the night
________ with envy a ________-bellied coward

LET'S TALK

Interview your classmates. Find out who prefers the old version of 'Little Red Riding Hood' and who prefers the new version. Which group wins? What were their reasons?

Use of English

Using verbs to tell stories

Storytellers use different versions of the past and present tenses to tell stories.

- Read the story 'Yi Shoots the Suns' aloud, with your partner.
- Pay attention to the verbs that are used. Which ones show actions that continue and which ones show actions that are completed?

Do you remember?

The past continuous tense describes an action that continues to happen in the past. It uses this form:

was/were + ________ing (form of the verb 'to be' + participle)

Try this

Work with your partner.

- Find all the past tense verbs in the frames. Write them down.
- Which of the actions was continuing in the past?
- Which of the actions was completed and finished?

PRACTISE

Complete these sentences by using the correct form of the verb in brackets. Write the answers in your notebook.

1. The suns (was/were) shining all at the same time.
2. This meant the Earth (was/were) drying up, and rivers (was/were) shrinking.
3. Emperor Yao was worried, because his people (was/were) dying.
4. He kept quiet about it, but he (was/were) making a plan.

Using connectives to join pieces of a story together

Try this

Continue reading the story about Yi and the suns.

- As you read, take note of all the connecting words and phrases. These are words and phrases that connect one frame to the next or one piece of action to the next.
- Make a list of these words and phrases in your notebook.

Do you remember?

Connectives are words that join sentences or parts of a story together. They are words and phrases like: as soon as, when, and so, although, but, however, etc.

PRACTISE

Join these sentences with the connecting words in brackets. Write the sentences in your notebook.

1. He said nothing to Yi. He was making a plan. (however)
2. Yao was a famous emperor. He was not too proud to ask for help. (although)
3. The suns agreed to shine one by one. The land would not dry up. (so that)
4. I will shoot all ten suns. The Earth will be saved. (and so)
5. My arrows are done. I will leave. (when)

Reading

Read about the oral tradition of storytelling

▲ A modern storyteller enchants an audience

▲ Griots in West Africa use music and drumming as part of their storytelling

Look at the photographs above and read the captions.

1 Talk about the photographs in your group.
   a Where do you think the story is being told in the first photograph?
   b What kind of people do you think are in the audience?
   c What is a '**griot**', do you think?

2 Read this information about storytelling around the world, then answer the questions that follow.

In times gone by, information was passed down from one **generation** to the next, through stories, usually told by older members of the family. Of course, this still happens today – you probably have someone in your family who insists on telling the same embarrassing story at every family gathering!
In my family, one of my aunts is the gatherer and keeper of all the family stories. She can tell you what my grandfather was doing in 1945. Well, almost!

Oral storytelling is an ancient tradition in many cultures. In West Africa, for example, the griots are honoured storytellers and advisors to kings. Not everyone can be a griot – it's an **hereditary** position, passed down from father to son, or mother to daughter. After dinner, the villagers all gather around a central fire, to listen to the griot tell tales of the past, often with a moral or message for the listeners.

The Hawaiian word for storytelling means 'the carrying of language'. The word for story is 'mo'olelo', from 'mo'o' meaning carrying or succession and 'olelo' which means language or speaking. So, the storyteller **literally** carries language from one generation to the next. Part of the role of the storyteller is to teach the next generation about Hawaiian traditions, as well as how to behave and what to value.

Irish storytellers moved from village to village bringing news, as well as telling old stories and **myths**. Sometimes, these myths were sung as songs and the listeners would join in on the choruses.

Aesop was one of the world's first recorded storytellers and his fables are still told today, 2500 years later. You know the stories of 'The Fox and the Crow' and 'The Fox and the Grapes'. Have you heard any other fables by Aesop?

Today, there's been a **revival** of storytelling, and many actors tell stories in theatres, at events and through social media. They use the power of their voices, but also song, movement and props to tell their stories.

a Which of the storytelling examples do you find most interesting?
b Do you know any other types of storytellers? Share what you know with the class.

Vocabulary

The table below contains words from the passage you have just read. Find the words in the passage. Can you tell from reading the words or sentences around them what the words mean?

- First, match the words with their meanings.
- Then, learn to spell the words.

Word	Meaning
embarrassing	very old
ancient	carrying
hereditary	all the people born at a particular time
succession	story
generation	passed down through the family
fable	coming back
revival	makes you feel awkward or ashamed

Now answer these questions.

1 What does 'oral storytelling' mean?
2 How do you think the writer feels about the stories her aunt tells?
3 If you live in West Africa, how do you become a griot?
4 How do people in West Africa feel about griots?
5 What does the Hawaiian word for storytelling mean?
6 What is similar between the stories of the Hawaiian storytellers and those of the griots?
7 Why do you think Aesop's stories are still told today?
8 What do modern storytellers use when they tell their stories?

DID YOU KNOW?
World Storytelling Day is held every year on 20 March. The day is a celebration of the oral storytelling tradition.

PRACTISE
Change these sentences from active to passive. For example:

People pass down information, over the years.

Information is passed down, over the years.

Write the passive sentences in your notebook.

1 A child starts the **ceremony**.
2 Someone lights the fire in the central area.
3 People tell stories around the fire at night.
4 An artist illustrates the stories.
5 The ticket seller sells tickets at the door to the theatre.

Do you remember?

In the active voice, the subject does the action. For example:

The storyteller told them about the dreamtime.

The youngest person asks the four questions.

In the passive voice, the action is being performed on the subject. For example:

The story is told.

Information is passed down through the generations.

The passive voice is used:

- when you don't need to say who does the action
- if you don't want to say who the subject is.

Speaking and listening

Listening to story reviews

1 Listen to Audio 3.4, a review of the story 'Cinderella'. Are you surprised to find out that this is not originally an English story? Listen carefully for the following information.

a In which other two cultures is this story told?

b Name two modern movies in which the Cinderella story has been used.

▲ Cinderella with the pumpkin

▲ A much older version of the Cinderella story is 'The Girl with the Rose Red Slippers'

LET'S TALK

Discuss these questions in your group.

1 What does the reviewer think about the story of Cinderella? Choose the correct answer.
   - a The story is old and good.
   - b The story is old and has been told too many times.
   - c Because the story is good, it has survived in different versions in different cultures.

2 What is the plot of the story? Choose the correct answer.
   - a Poor girl or boy marries a prince or princess, lives happily ever after.
   - b Hard work pays off; if you work hard you can marry a princess or prince.
   - c Everyone has a fairy godmother who can help them.

3 Do you know a similar story? What is it called?

4 You are going to write and then present a review of a traditional tale. Look at the writing frame on the next page. Discuss it with your group. You can use this frame when you write the review.

Review of:

Source (newspaper, radio, etc.):

Target audience:

Paragraph 1: Who are the characters and where is the story set?

Paragraph 2: Does it have a good plot? (Don't give away the ending!)

Paragraph 3: Say whether or not this was a good story, and why. Also, say whether you recommend people read it/listen to it or not.

2 Listen to Audio 3.5, the story of 'The Boy who Cried "Wolf!"'

As you listen, make notes so you can write and present a review of the story.

▶ If you lie too often, people will never believe you when you tell the truth

Try this

Using your frame, write a short review of the story.

- Bring your review to class, and be prepared to present it to the class.
- Be ready to argue your point of view if someone disagrees with your review.

CHALLENGE YOURSELF

Write a review of another story you know. Say what you liked or didn't like about it.

Writing

Write your own story

Try this

Choose one of your favourite traditional tales and rewrite it:
- in a modern setting
- OR from a different character's points of view.

Here is a checklist for writing your story. Begin by planning your story, with a mind map or a diagram. Then, use this checklist to help you.

Planning
- Use a mind map or diagram.
- Each main idea becomes a paragraph.
- Each paragraph has a topic sentence.
- Each topic sentence is followed by supporting sentences.

Structure
- There are two or three main characters.
- An action happens – there is a problem or crisis to solve.
- There is an ending, where the problem is solved.
- There could be a moral to the story, but it's not essential.

Sentences
- All sentences are properly constructed.
- All sentences are punctuated correctly.
- Sentences are varied (some questions, some statements, a few exclamations, etc.).

Words
- All words are spelled correctly.
- All words are right for this kind of story.
- The vocabulary used is interesting.

Ask a friend to check your story for language and spelling errors. Then, write or type out a neat copy to hand in to your teacher.

Self check

- Have you used narrative tenses to write your story – the simple past and the past continuous?
- Is the story brought to life with adjectives and comparisons?
- Have you used connecting words to join paragraphs and the pieces of action in the story?

CHALLENGE YOURSELF

As a class, put together a Stage 8 storybook. This could be something you sell to raise funds for a favourite charity.

- Collect all your stories and have a neat copy typed out.
- Illustrate your stories.
- Your teacher will help to get the stories copied and bound, so you can sell the book to family and friends.

What can you do?

Read and review what you can do.

- I can listen to traditional tales and a film review.
- I can talk about modern tales, traditional tales and the tradition of storytelling.
- I can read traditional stories and fairy tales.
- I can write my own story from a different point of view.
- I can use past tenses, adjectives, connectives and the active and passive voice to write an extended text.

Now you have completed Unit 3, you may like to try the Unit 3 online knowledge test if you are using the Boost eBook.

Review Units 1–3

PRACTISE

Use words from the box to complete these sentences.

fluent	bilingual	rid	mobile	declutter
hereditary	drones	**permanent**	broaden	storytellers

1 My sister and I both speak Malay and we are ______________ in English as well.

2 Everyone should learn at least one other language so that they can be ______________.

3 You have too many shoes. You need to get ______________ of some!

4 They have moved around so much but now they have a ______________ home.

5 Can ______________ be used to deliver packages? I know they are used to take photographs.

6 Learning a new language can ______________ your mind and help you understand another culture.

7 They live in a ______________ home that is easy to pack up and move around.

8 The role of a storyteller is often a ______________ one, so stories pass from one generation to the next.

9 Before you move to a new house, you will need to ______________.

10 Griots are honoured ______________ and advisors to kings in West Africa.

HINT
Use the correct intonation as you read the statements, questions and exclamations.

Try this

Work in pairs and complete the conversation. Use the correct forms of the given words. When you are sure of the correct words, read the conversation aloud. (You will each need to read two parts.)

Lee: What do you think our living spaces (will look like/will be looking like) in the future?

Fabio: If I knew I (will/would) tell you!

Anil: I think our homes will be (built/build) by 3D printers.

Nikki: Yes, maybe. I (were/was) reading about that yesterday. The article said that if we (didn't find/didn't found) cheaper ways of building, housing would be even more of a problem than it is now.

Fabio: I don't like the idea of a printed home (very much/much very)! What happens when it rains?

Anil: The printing (be done/is done) with concrete, not paper!

Nikki: I think our spaces (are going/will) to be greener. People today (understands/understand) the importance of plants.

Lee: Yes, everyone has started to realise that (slowest/slowly). I hope it isn't too late!

PRACTISE

Can you write these sentences correctly? You will need to choose the correct words to do this.

1. If I (speak/spoke) Spanish, I would be able to understand what they are saying!
2. When (is going/will/shall) the storyteller start telling the story?
3. You speak so many languages, will you teach me (one/that)?
4. (None/No one) in my family can speak Arabic.
5. He (shares/share) a room with his brothers.
6. All my possessions (is packing/are packed) away neatly in the cupboard now.
7. Our apartment is (on/up) the second floor.
8. Red and Gran (were hiding/have hided) in the cupboard when the Wolf knocked on the door.
9. The river (dry/dried) up and the trees died.
10. She speaks Portuguese and English, but she wants to learn another language (although/so that) she can be multilingual.

LET'S TALK

Work in small groups. Look at the photographs below and read the captions. Then use the internet to find out what each story is about. Choose one of the stories and tell it to the rest of the class. Work out how each person in the group can participate in the storytelling. Use intonation to make your story sound exciting.

▲ Sculpture of 'The Lion and the Mouse', a fable by Aesop, in the Netherlands

▲ Painting of the story 'The man who sold his coat', another of Aesop's fables

PRACTISE

In Unit 2, you worked in groups to design your ideal living space for the future. You drew plans and then wrote a report about your project. What did you learn from the project? Did it change your ideas about your living space?

Draft a short report of two paragraphs. You can use the following structure:

- Paragraph 1: Explain briefly what sort of living space your group designed.
- Paragraph 2: Give your opinion about the design. Did it help you to form a better idea about living spaces? What did you learn?

You can publish your report on your school website, social media page or newspaper.

CHALLENGE YOURSELF

Write a magazine article in which you explain why you think it is important or not important to speak more than one language.

4 Advertising

In this unit you will:

- listen to a podcast, an interview and a sales story about **advertising**
- talk about how emotions are used in advertising, and make a **pitch** to sell something
- read about **viral** advertising **campaigns** and do a survey
- write your own advertisement
- use the present perfect tense, prepositional and phrasal verbs, the infinitive and gerunds, and abstract and compound nouns.

Speaking and listening

Appealing to your emotions

1 How do advertisers convince us to buy things? Discuss this in your group.
- Can you remember an advertisement that you liked a lot?
- Why did you like the advertisement?
- What emotions did it make you feel?
- Did you, or your parents, buy the product that was advertised?
- Which of these emotions have you felt, when you look at advertisements?

envy	desire	fear	happiness	anger

- Can you think of specific advertisements that have made you feel these emotions?

2 Listen to Audio 4.1, a radio interview with an advertising expert. Look at the photographs on the opposite page as you listen.

a Write down the emotions you think of for each product in the pictures. Choose from this list.

fear disgust love envy desire need hope faith happiness togetherness pride

b Do you agree with what the interviewer says about using these specific emotions to sell the products?

c Do you think that different emotions were used? Discuss this in your group.

d Have you bought any products like these?

e What made you buy these products?

Do you remember?

Words like fear, envy, happiness and love are all abstract nouns. They name a feeling or an emotion, and not a physical thing.

Try this

Many verbs are used with prepositions. There are several examples in the interview you have just listened to. Choose the correct preposition to go with these verbs.

out	to	in	into	of	from	for	on

1 Let's get ______ the subject straight away.
2 What I really want to find ______ , is how they use your emotions.
3 They try to scare you ______ buying their product.
4 Think ______ reasons why this might not be true.
5 They have been waiting ______ trainers for a while now.

Speaking and listening

Listen to a success story about juice

Listen to Audio 4.2, a podcast about how Zesty Morning Fruit Juice spread their advertising message to their customers – and gained new customers too. Before you listen, discuss these questions in your group.

1 How do you feel in the morning as you wake up and prepare for school? Do you feel different on weekday and weekend mornings?
2 Try to name each of the moods you think the faces are expressing in the pictures below. Which of these do you feel in the morning?
3 Which of these moods and feelings are mentioned in the audio? Discuss this with your group.

Slow	Excited	Tired	Sad	Angry
Confused	Sluggish	Happy	Energised	Sleepy

Try this

Talk about these questions on the Zesty Morning Fruit Juice podcast (Audio 4.2) with a partner.

1 How did Zesty Morning Fruit Juice come up with the idea for the 'Zesty Morning' advertising campaign?
2 What did they discover about people's online behaviour?
3 How did they use this knowledge to build an advertising campaign?
4 Look at the faces above and the print advertisement opposite. Why do you think these particular colours are used?
5 Do you think this is an effective advertisement? Why or why not?

PRACTISE

Practise using the language of advertising in your group.

1 What is a 'brand'? Find three brand names in the photos in this unit.
2 What is a '**tag line**'? Find two examples in the photographs.
3 Do you know any other tag lines for brands?
4 What is a 'logo'? Find three examples.
5 How would you describe what an advertising campaign is?
6 Who or what is a '**target market**'?

Try this

Complete these sentences by adding a phrasal verb from the box.

1 We are going to __________ which slogan to use in our advertising campaign.
2 We need to __________ with a really catchy slogan.
3 It is time to __________ and think of new ways to attract younger customers.
4 When our target market __________ about our new sneakers, we sold out in just one day!

come up	look ahead	work out	found out

CHALLENGE YOURSELF

Choose an advertisement that you like. Do some research on it at home. Come to your next class prepared to do a short talk about:

- what is being advertised
- the target market
- the brand name and tag line
- why you think this is a successful advertisement.

Use of English

Present perfect tense

Talk about the words in this picture. All of these words are used in advertising.

- Do you understand each word? Discuss their meanings with your group and look up any that you don't understand. Write the words and their meanings in your notebook.
- Learn to spell the words.

Do you remember?

Present perfect tense

The present perfect tense describes an action that has finished, but is still connected to the present. For example:

They have interviewed the people to find out what social media they use.

He has worked in advertising for the last three years.

Present perfect = auxiliary + past participle
= has/have + verb ending in -ed

PRACTISE

Use the correct form of the verbs in brackets. Write the sentences in your notebook.

1 The movie came out last week, but I (have/has) already (to see) it.
2 They (have/has) (to struggle) to find actors for the commercial.
3 We (have/has) (to do) the research; we are ready to plan the campaign now.
4 I (have/has) (to forget) my **portfolio**, I will have to go and fetch it.
5 You (have/has) not (to see) the advertisement yet, have you?
6 They (have/has) (to be) to the office to fetch the script.
7 Your lack of interest in the project (have/has) (to worry) me.
8 I (have/has) (to want) to see that commercial for a long time!

Try this

Read this survey about online advertising. Talk about the questions with your partner and then write your own answers in your notebook.

1 What form of advertising do you think is the most effective?
   a I have always liked online advertising.
   b Print advertising has been my favourite for years.
   c I have listened to the radio for most of my life, so I prefer radio ads.
2 How would you describe online advertising?
   a It has always annoyed me, the way it pops up into your feed, without you asking for it to be there.
   b I have found it very useful and informative.
   c I don't think it's useful, it has worried me for a long time – how do they know exactly what you are interested in?
3 Do you ever 'like' posts on social media from a brand you enjoy?
   a Yes, I have done so often.
   b No, I have never liked a branded post.
4 If you see a friend like a post or a brand, would you go to visit that brand's page?
   a In the past, I have done so, but it wasn't worth my time.
   b Yes, if it is a brand that I like.
5 How often do you buy products because you have seen them advertised online or discounted online?
   a I **rarely** buy products online; I have done in the past, but I've had to return them, because they are the wrong size, or they don't look like what was advertised at all.
   b I love buying online; it saves so much time.

Compare your answers to your partner's.

- Do you have the same opinions about online shopping?
- Where do your opinions differ?

CHALLENGE YOURSELF

Find all the examples of the present perfect tense in the online survey. Write them in your notebook. For example, the first one is:

I have always liked online advertising.

Work with your partner. Use your list of verbs to ask each other questions. For example:

Q: Have you ever liked a branded post?

A: No, I've never liked a branded post.

Work with a partner and from memory, write down the main points of the discussion about Zesty Morning Fruit Juice and their 'Zesty Morning' campaign.

- Compare your points to another pair's. Have you left anything out?

Reading

Read about an unusual advertising campaign

1 Discuss these questions in your group.
   - a What do you like or dislike about fast food? What is your favourite fast food meal?
   - b Why do you prefer that fast food?
   - c Does advertising have anything to do with it or not?
   - d Quick as you can, list all the fast food places that advertise in your area.

2 Read about a different approach to advertising.
   - a As you read, think about the kind of language used in this extract. Is it formal English? Is it more casual English?
   - b Think about this advertising campaign. Does it make you like McDonald's better?
   - c Does it convince you that McDonald's cares about the environment? Is the advertising good, because it's eco-friendly? Do you think it might be more effective because it's something different?

International fast food company McDonald's released an unusual kind of advertising campaign. Sean Click, the designer, has found a sneaky way of getting the McDonald's logo onto the side of the highway, in California, without paying for a billboard.

How? He has used a concept known as 'seed bombing'. Sean has planted seeds for bright yellow poppies in the familiar shape of the McDonald's 'M'. The seeds have blossomed into some natural advertising for the fast food brand.

Cool, right? What is even more clever, is that Sean's used California wild poppies. These poppies are the state flower for California, and therefore it is **illegal** to dig them up or damage them. This advert was impossible to get rid of, or to hide, without planting more flowers.

This is an example of advertising that is good for the environment, cost effective and very clever.

▲ California wild poppy seeds were sown in the shape of an M

Let's hope this branch of eco-advertising continues to grow!

Register is using language differently according to who you are speaking or writing to.

For example, in a formal register you would write:

It's impressive what Sean has managed to achieve.

In the less formal or more casual register used in this piece, the writer says:

Cool, right?

Vocabulary

Answer these multiple-choice questions in your notebook.

1 How would you normally advertise on the side of a motorway?
 a on a billboard
 b on a flyer
 c in a campaign

2 What does 'has found a sneaky way' mean?
 a has told on someone
 b has found a clever solution
 c has found a back road

3 Seed bombing is
 a dropping seeds from an aeroplane
 b planting seeds secretly
 c making small bombs out of seeds.

4 The poppies can't be removed because
 a it has been stated
 b they are the state flower, and it's illegal to dig them up
 c they have flowered into an advertising campaign.

5 Eco-advertising means
 a advertising in a way that does not harm the environment
 b advertising economically
 c advertising that is cost effective.

6 Match the words in box A with their opposites in box B.

A

international	unusual	illegal
fast	familiar	impossible
new	natural	intelligent

B

ordinary	possible	manufactured
local	slow	old
stupid	strange	legal

Do you remember?

We use the prefixes un-, il- and im- to make words with opposite meanings. All these prefixes mean 'not'.

7 Change these words to their opposites, by using a prefix from the box.

un-	il-	im-	inter

 a national
 b usual
 c legal
 d possible
 e natural
 f familiar

8 Learn to spell the new words that you made.

LET'S TALK

Do you have any billboards in your town?

- Which is your favourite billboard advertisement, and why?
- What products are advertised on the billboards?
- What do you notice about the amount of text and the pictures used on a billboard?

Use of English

Talking about advertising

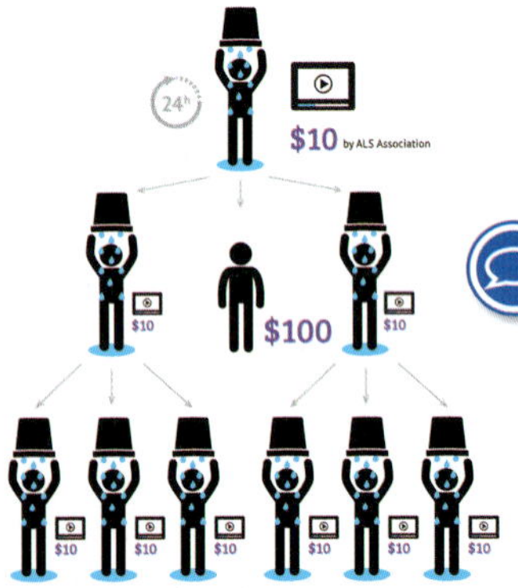

ALS ICE BUCKET CHALLENGE

is an activity involving dumping a bucket of ice water on someone's head to promote awareness of the disease amyotrophic lateral sclerosis (ALS) and encourage donations to research.

CONGRATULATIONS!
YOU ARE BEING CHALLENGED!

- record a video of yourself pouring bucket of ice water over your head
- call out a challenge to three other people
- donate $10 by the ALS Association

OR

donate $100 by the ALS Association

PRACTISE

1 Put the verbs in brackets into the present perfect tense. Write the sentences in your notebook. For example:

He (use) poppy seeds.	He has used poppy seeds.

a A fast food company (release) their latest campaign.
b The designer (find) a sneaky way to advertise the logo.
c He (use) a concept called 'seed bombing'.
d He (plant) seeds in the shape of an M.
e The seeds (blossom) and grown.
f This (be) one of the most unusual advertising campaigns ever.

2 Work with a partner. First read this dialogue out loud with each other. Each of you can be one of the speakers.

Shafika: Have you heard about the #IceBucketChallenge?
Tariq: Something about celebrities dumping ice over themselves? Where did you find out about it?
Shafika: One of my friends works for the ALS Association. The #IceBucketChallenge raised millions of dollars, and it wasn't even started by an advertising agency! Some friends made a video challenging each other to dump a bucket of ice over their heads, and it grew from there.
Tariq: Well, it's great that they raised so much money for charity. What does ALS stand for?
Shafika: Amyotrophic Lateral Sclerosis. It's a horrible disease that kills off your neurons, and your nerves eventually die.
Tariq: That sounds terrible. I know that Bill Gates, Lady Gaga and Justin Timberlake all took part in the challenge.
Shafika: And Selena Gomez. I didn't run across them, but I did the challenge too! That water was *sooooo* cold! But it was worth it to help raise funds.

3 Now, working with your partner, find all of these prepositional verbs in the dialogue.

take part	stand for	hear about
grow from	work for	start by

4 Finally, work on your own to make sentences with the prepositional verbs from activity 3. Write the sentences in your notebook.

More language about advertising

A gerund is a verbal noun. Gerunds have the ending -ing, and they describe an action.

Here are some gerunds: running, sailing, acting, advertising.

- You can use gerunds after certain nouns like enjoy, like, dislike, keep, finish, recommend and avoid. For example:

I like running, she dislikes running; but we both enjoy sailing.

- You can also use gerunds after prepositions of place and time. For example:

We need to make a decision before advertising the position.

The infinitive is the form of the verb with 'to' + the root verb.

Here are some infinitives: to run, to sail, to act, to advertise. For example:

We need to advertise the product online.

You can use an infinitive or a gerund, depending on the structure of a sentence.

PRACTISE

1 Use a gerund from the box to complete this dialogue. Work with a partner.

sailing	advertising	drawing	dancing	performing

Tomas: How do you know you want to do __________ when you leave school?

Anna: Well, I love art, and __________, so I thought it would be a good creative job for me.

Tomas: I could never sit in an office all day. Can one make a living out of __________?

Anna: I think so. You won't get rich! __________ in public is not my strength.

Tomas: Well, my only other interest is __________, and no one will pay me for that!

2 Complete these sentences in your notebook. Use the infinitive form of the verb in brackets.

a I'm going (do) the #IceBucketChallenge next year with my class.
b You get (dump) a bucket of ice water on someone's head.
c Then you have (record) yourself doing this.
d And you have (challenge) three other people (do) it too.
e This is a good way (raise) money.

3 Choose to use the infinitive form of the verb, or a gerund, to complete these sentences.

a My sister chose (work) in advertising.
b She loves (read) about interesting advertising campaigns around the world.
c I don't know yet what I want (do) after school.
d Do you mind (help) me with this test?
e (Graduate) top of the class would be first prize!

CHALLENGE YOURSELF

Using the picture on the previous page and the text in the dialogue, explain to your partner how the #IceBucketChallenge works. Use these questions to help you.

- What is the aim of the challenge?
- What do people have to do?
- How do they make money from doing it?

▲ The Great Dress Debate

Reading

Going viral

1 Did you ever see, read or hear about the online argument about whether the colour of a particular dress was white and gold, or black and blue? Look at the photograph. Discuss it in your group.

a What colour do you think the dress is?

b Why do you think an argument like this would go viral?

c Why do you think anyone would care about this at all?

2 Read about how clever advertisers have watched things go viral on social media and then used the chance to advertise their product. We'll start with that dress!

DID YOU KNOW?

'Go viral' means that something spreads rapidly and uncontrollably, like a virus. To 'go viral' in this sense, means something is posted on social media, like Facebook, Twitter or TikTok, and then gets quickly shared so many times that suddenly it seems like the whole world is talking about it.

Online advertising campaigns often go viral when they respond quickly to something that's **popular** at the time. 'Go viral' means spreading very quickly, as you know. In 2015, there was an online argument about the colour of a dress, which, to some, looked white and gold, and, to others, looked black and blue. The laundry detergent brand Tide sent out a tweet saying 'Looks like a problem when you don't use Tide Plus ColorGuard'. The tweet had over 10,000 retweets! This was a very clever response to the argument that was happening in social media because when the response got retweeted, over 10,000 people saw the Tide brand.

▲ Tide used the online argument to feature their product

Another example is a filmmaker who was trying to help his girlfriend sell her car. He made a video advertisement and posted it on Twitter. The video went viral, because it showed his girlfriend in her car, with her cat, drinking coffee, looking cool and confident. It was very cleverly done.

A company called CarMax responded to the video by releasing their own video offering to buy the car, but also the items in the filmmaker's video, including the Mexican coffee mug, his girlfriend's fluffy jacket and even their cat!

Amazon is a company that sells books and other products, and delivers to your door, once you place an order online. Jeep is a company making **off-road** vehicles, for use on rough, gravel roads. If you own a Jeep, you are probably an adventurous type of person, who takes different roads – not the usual smooth roads that most people drive on.

Amazon and Jeep got together with the moviemakers who created the new 'Jurassic World' movie. They made an advertising campaign together, to **promote** their brands and the release of the new film.

To create excitement and interest, they delivered a giant Amazon box using a truck and a Jeep **motorcade**, and dropped the box in the middle of a busy shopping mall. The box was covered in **hashtags** and had air holes punched in it. What was inside? A dinosaur? People went wild about this campaign – an Amazon delivery 65 million years in the making!

LG is a company that makes appliances for your home, like washing machines. At a four-day music festival called Bannaroo in the USA, LG set up an area called 'The LaundROO Lounge', where festival visitors could get their clothes washed, dried and folded for free. LG was very popular with these festival goers!

Vocabulary

1 Answer these questions.
  - **a** What is the company Tide **implying** when they say 'Looks like a problem when you don't use Tide Plus ColorGuard'?
  - **b** What emotions does the CarMax's viral campaign make you feel?
  - **c** If you were old enough, would you buy a car from CarMax? Why or why not?
  - **d** What emotions is the Jurassic World advertisement playing on?
  - **e** Why do you think LG targeted young people at a music festival? Most of them probably don't even own their own washing machines yet.
  - **f** How do you feel about advertisers using other people's stories to promote their products?
  - **g** Would you allow an advertiser to use your life story to promote their product? Why or why not?

2 There are many compound nouns in this unit. See how many you can make from the words in the box.

maker	high	office	way
bill	box	star	line
girl	film	fire	on
wild	movie	friend	board.

3 Choose five of your compound nouns and use them in sentences of your own. Write your sentences in your notebook.

Speaking and listening

Listen to a home-grown story

Listen to Audio 4.3, the story of how Organic Valley started. As you listen, think about these questions.

1 How does the advertising for Organic Valley differ from the advertising you have learned about in the rest of this unit?

2 Would the advertising make you buy products from Organic Valley? Why or why not?

LET'S TALK

Discuss these questions in your group.

1 What is the story of Organic Valley?
2 What do you know about 'hippies' or nature-lovers?
3 What was different about this group of hippies?
4 When did they start the farming **co-operative?**
5 What was their goal?
6 Name three things that have changed for this group in the last 30 years.
7 What has not changed?
8 Do you think using the story of Organic Valley is successful advertising, or not? Explain your answer.
9 What does this statement mean: 'Your company values can set you apart from the competition'?
10 Do you believe this argument is true for Organic Valley?

Try this

Find the abstract nouns in these sentences. Write them in your notebook.

1 Sometimes truth is the best advertising tool there is.
2 I know I won't make a lot of money, but I still have hope!
3 Success comes to those who work hard.
4 You can learn things from failure too.
5 I don't think advertising is a business where you will find fame and glory.

CHALLENGE YOURSELF

Have a look at the Organic Valley website (www.organicvalley.coop/about-us/). Click on the button that says 'Watch our crazy video'. Discuss the video in your groups.

1 What do you think the values of Organic Valley are?
2 How do you feel about people who can sustain their beliefs for 30 years?
3 Did you like seeing the young people, and comparing them to what they are now?
4 What lesson can you learn from this group of people?
5 Which section of the advertisement did you like best, and why?
6 Was there any part of the advertisement that you felt did not work? Explain which part, and why you did not think it worked.

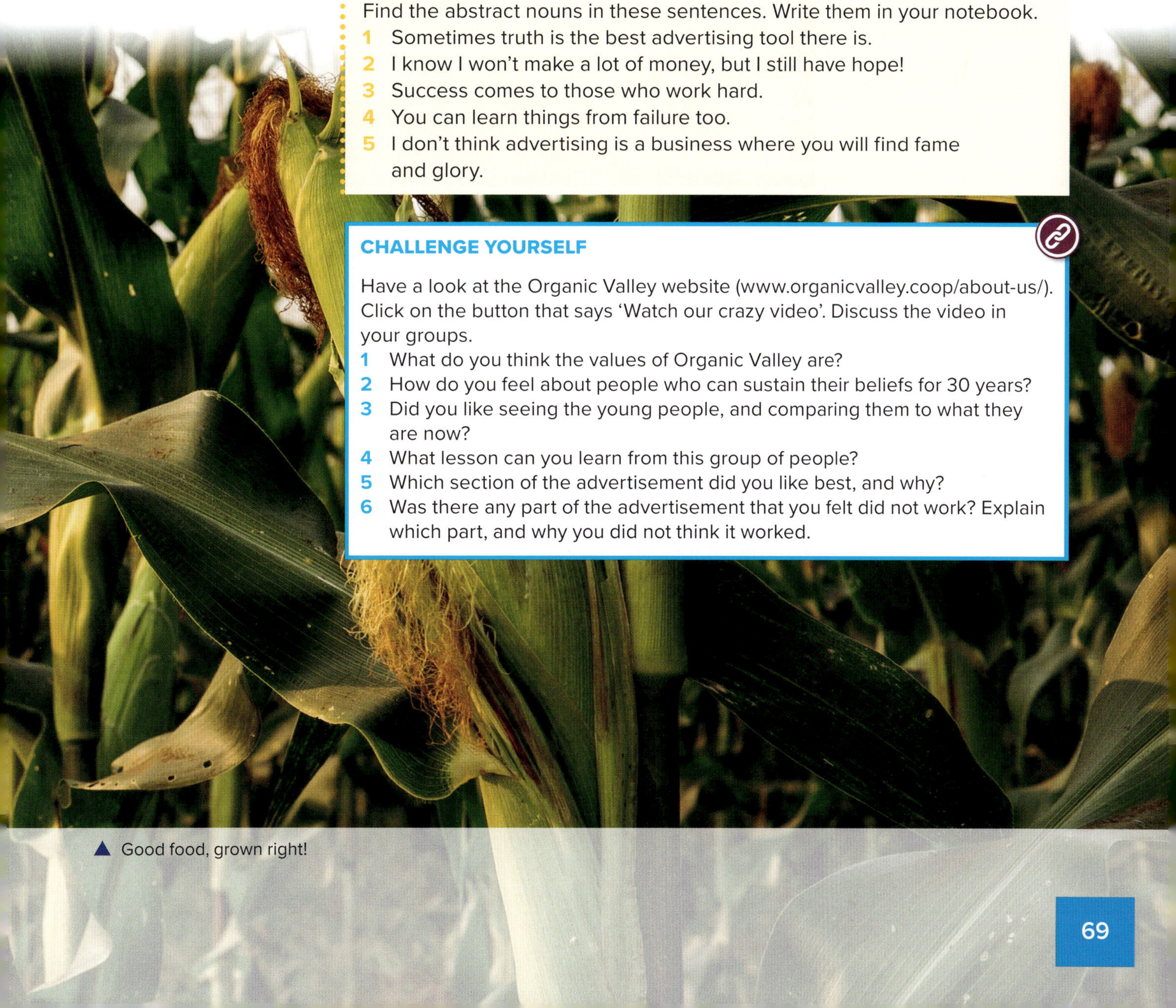

▲ Good food, grown right!

Writing

Create an advertisement

▲ Now it's time to design your own advertisement, for a product you really like

Try this

Design your own advertisement, to sell a real or imagined product, using only:

- the brand name
- a tag line
- an image
- one short paragraph.

You are going to send your advertisement out via email, to your group, who will vote on the best advertisement.

STEP 1: First make notes on:

- who your target market is
- how you will get their attention
- how you can use emotion to persuade them to buy your product.

STEP 2:

- Sketch a rough copy of your design in your notebook.
- Look online for photographs or images to use in your advertisement. Try Adobe Stock or Shutterstock; they have a range of different images you might like to use. Or take your own photograph to use in your advertisement.
- Get a friend to proofread your writing before you make a final, neat copy.

HINT

Try to use prepositional verbs and the present perfect in your advertisement if you can. If not, focus on other useful grammar from this unit – compound nouns, abstract nouns, gerunds or infinitives.

CHALLENGE YOURSELF

Write an advertisement for the story book you made in Unit 3. Decide how much you will sell the book for and to whom. Where will the proceeds go?

You can either make print posters to advertise the books for sale or do an email campaign and send out your email to the schools mailing list – with your head teacher's approval, of course!

Self check

In your group, evaluate each other's advertisements.

- How many people in your group would buy your product?
- Vote for the best product and the best advertisement.
- Who sold their product most effectively? Discuss why.
- Write up a list of your group's findings about what makes a successful advertisement.

What can you do?

Read and review what you can do.

- I can listen to a podcast, an interview and a sales story about advertising.
- I can talk about how emotions are used in advertising, and make a pitch to sell something.
- I can read about viral advertising campaigns and do a survey.
- I can write my own advertisement.
- I can use the present perfect tense, prepositional and phrasal verbs, the infinitive and gerunds, and abstract and compound nouns.

Now you have completed Unit 4, you may like to try the Unit 4 online knowledge test if you are using the Boost eBook.

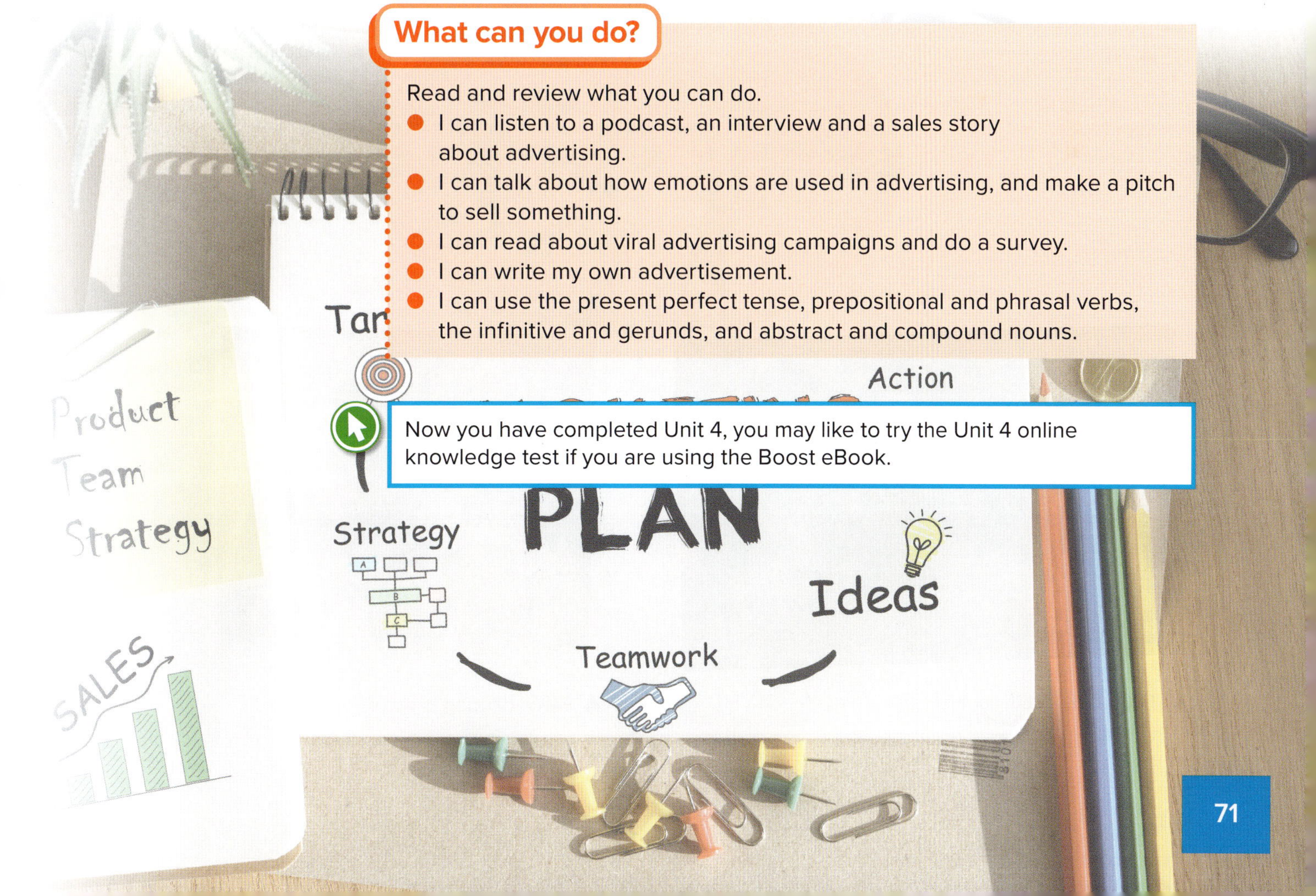

5 Music connects us

In this unit you will:

- listen to opinions about why music is important
- talk about music and its importance
- read about how music can break down barriers and about music festivals
- write an email or a message describing a music festival
- use present perfect tenses and relative clauses
- use punctuation to make text clear and easy to read
- Project: plan a music festival.

▲ Rap artists

▲ Musicians playing music on a street

◀ A folk festival

▲ The Mzansi Youth choir

▲ Break-dancing is part of hip-hop

Speaking and listening

Music we like

1 Work in small groups. Talk about the music that you enjoy.
   a What type of music do you like listening to?
   b Where and how do you listen to this type of music?
   c How does music make you feel? Relaxed, happy, energetic, sad?

2 Look at the pictures on the opposite page. Then, listen to Audio 5.1, a short talk which gives more information about different genres of music. Match each **genre** to one of the pictures.

HINT

There are many different styles or genres of music. Here are a few:

Classical Rock Punk Rock Pop K-Pop Folk Country
Rhythm and Blues (R&B) Reggae Funk Hip-hop Techno
Jazz Singing Rap Disco Folk

PRACTISE

1 Work in pairs. Listen to the talk again and read the names of the different styles or genres of music in the HINT box.

2 Choose one genre that you like and tell your partner something about that genre. Try to make five or six sentences. Start like this:

I love hip-hop. Hip-hop ...

3 Listen to your partner's talk. Then ask your partner two questions about the genre. For example:

Which band plays this music? Who is your favourite singer?

HINT

It doesn't matter if you make some mistakes when you talk. Focus on using the correct vocabulary first. Then help each other to correct mistakes.

Try this

Work with a partner. Find out about one of the other music genres mentioned in the HINT box. Write down notes and give a very short talk to the class about this genre. Your talk should take about one minute. Try to include examples of bands or singers who perform this style of music.

Speaking and listening

Music helped me connect

Someone once said, 'Music expresses what you don't know how to say!' Maybe this is why so many people find that music helps them to connect with other people. It doesn't really matter what kind of music you like to listen to.

1 Listen to the two short talks in Audio 5.2. Both of them express opinions about how music has helped people to connect with others.

2 Listen to what Darryl says again. Which of these statements can you use to summarise what Darryl feels about music?

- a Darryl does not like music very much.
- b He loved the first pop concert he went to.
- c He feels that he is part of a group because he enjoyed music with other people.
- d He doesn't think that music is important.
- e He still wears the T-shirt from the concert because it makes him feel part of a group.
- f Music has helped Darryl to feel that he **belongs** in a group.

3 Listen to what Meena says again. Which of these statements can you use to summarise what Meena feels about music?

- a Music has changed Meena's life.
- b Meena has had many changes in her life **recently**.
- c Meena is shy and she finds it difficult to speak to people she doesn't know.
- d Meena loves music.
- e Meena shares her music with other students at school and in this way she has made new friends.
- f Meena has no new friends in the community.

HINT

To **belong** to a group means to feel as if you are part of a group and to feel accepted by that group.

Try this

1 Work in groups. Talk about what Meena and Darryl said about music. They both gave their opinions about why music was important in their lives.

2 Vote on the following statements. Do you agree or disagree?

- Enjoying music with other people helps you feel as if you belong to a group.
- It is important to feel as if you belong to a group.
- Music is something you can share with other people.
- Music is a good way to start a conversation.
- A conversation can lead to a new friendship.

3 Present the results of your votes to the rest of the class. Here are some phrases you could use:

Most of the group ...

Half of the group ...

A few people in the group ...

No one in the group ...

DID YOU KNOW?

Some scientists think they have proved that music helps plants to grow better. Maybe that's why some people sing to their plants!

Many people also believe that we work and study better if we listen to music at the same time. What do you think? What kind of music do you think would be best to listen to while studying? How could you make a fair test to prove any of these ideas? What would you have to do?

PRACTISE

Work in pairs. Role-play these scenes. Then choose one and role-play it for the class.

SCENE A

You have been to a pop concert. You meet someone from your class who was also at the concert. Greet each other. Then talk about the concert. Ask and answer questions about:

- where the concert was (the venue)
- the performers
- what you enjoyed
- what you did at the concert.

SCENE B

You are new at a school. You sit next to someone at break and start a conversation about music. Then you offer to share some music you have with the person you meet. After that, ask a few more questions to get to know the person. Swap roles too.

CHALLENGE YOURSELF

Find out one or two interesting facts or beliefs about music and tell your class about them.

Use of English

Unfinished actions

Do you remember?

We use the present perfect tense to describe unfinished past actions. These are actions that we started or did in the recent past and that we are still doing or hope to continue doing in the future. The actions in the past have direct links to things that still happen in the present.

Try this

Work in pairs. You listened to Darryl and Meena talk about how music has helped them to connect with other people. Now, think about the verb tenses they used and why they used them.

- Darryl used the present perfect tense in this sentence: 'Music has helped me to feel that I belong.' (He didn't say: 'Music helped me to feel that I belong.') Why did he use this tense?
- Meena said that moving to London 'has been a big change for me.' Why did she use the present perfect tense? How do we form the present perfect tense?

We often use present perfect tenses with adverbs that express indefinite time. For example:

My family has <u>recently</u> moved to London.

They have lived here <u>since</u> 2019.

Have you <u>ever</u> watched Beyoncé perform on stage?

PRACTISE

Choose the correct form of the verb in each sentence or question. Write the complete correct sentence in your notebook.

1. Music (has/have helped) me to make friends.
2. Hip-hop (has been popular/has being popular) since the 1970s.
3. Meena (has be living/has been living) here for a few months.
4. Darryl (has worn/has wear) his pop concert T-shirt many times.
5. Have you ever (listened/listening) to hip-hop?
6. Meera (recently has found/has recently found) that music helps her to make friends.
7. (Have you ever tried/Have you never try) break-dancing? It's not easy!
8. My father (have ever heard/has never heard) of Gangnam Style!

Try this

Work in pairs. Ask and answer questions about music that you have listened to. Use:

- recently
- ever/never
- yet.

Relative clauses link

Do you remember?

Relative clauses are clauses that begin with relative pronouns such as who, that, which, whom, when, why and whose. The pronouns link the clauses.

Can you identify the relative pronouns in these sentences?

1 Angelique Tidjo is the singer who is the most well known in West Africa.
2 My grandfather, who is 93, loves hip-hop music.
3 Classical music is something that I have always enjoyed.
4 We went to a concert which was completely sold out!
5 I remember when I first heard Beyoncé sing!
6 He doesn't remember where the concert was advertised.

Relative pronouns can also be used with prepositions. For example:

to whom, from whom, with which, on which, from where

Here are some examples.

Jo is a person for whom music has always been very important.

The family moved from where they had lived for many years, to a country where they knew nobody.

The aunt from whom I got the violin lives in Japan.

In the examples above, 'whom' is used in a formal way. When people talk, they express the same ideas using 'who' like this:

Jo is a person who has always thought that music is very important.

The aunt who gave me the violin lives in Japan.

PRACTISE

Choose the best relative pronoun to complete each sentence.

1 My cousin, (who/whom) is only six, is already a great musician.
2 I find it difficult to talk to people (which/whom) I don't know.
3 I come from a town (why/where) people love to dance and sing.
4 The shop (from which/that from) I bought the microphone, is every expensive.
5 The phone (on which/on who) I play my music is very **precious** to me.
6 Do you remember (when/that) you first heard rap music?

Try this

In formal writing and speech we often connect clauses by using a preposition (from, on, to, with) with a relative pronoun (whom, which). Work in pairs and try connecting these clauses. You will need to choose a preposition and a relative pronoun to connect the clauses.

Share your sentences with the class afterwards.

What is the name of the website?	I go to buy milk and bread.
This is the street	she learned how to play a tune.
The shop is down the road	I got the information about the festival.
This is a guitar	you can buy and download music.
The person is my cousin	we are going to the festival.
What is the type of transport	the Lee family moved.

Reading

> **HINT**
> A 'barrier' is something that stops you from doing something. A fence or a gate are barriers that can stop you from going somewhere, for example.

What's your opinion?

We all face barriers in our lives. Sometimes the barriers are those which are created by money or lack of money. Barriers that have to do with class, religion or health are also common. Sometimes we just feel that there are barriers everywhere, like when you move to a new country or a new house and you have to go to a different school.

1 What do you think? What barriers do you face in your life right now?
2 Work alone and write down three ideas. (You do not need to share these ideas.)
3 Many people believe that music can help to break down the barriers that we face. Read what some people have to say about this. Do you agree or disagree?

Text A: Shyness

People face different barriers. You will remember the story about Meera, for whom **shyness** was a barrier. She didn't find it easy to talk to people who she didn't know. She moved from her school and country, where she had many friends, to a new place where she hardly knew anyone. So she had to find a way to make new friends. She had to **overcome** her shyness. She did this by sharing her music with others.

Text B: Health

I live with a condition called Asperger syndrome. It's a condition that makes me feel **anxious** at times. It can be a barrier for me because I find it difficult to socialise with other people and to make friends. This is because I don't recognise how other people feel. But I have found a way to overcome this barrier. I have joined a choir which allows me to perform. And I love performing for an audience! I have never felt as happy and confident before. Our choir has won competitions too. So now I believe that music can break down barriers.

Text C: Gender and race

Aretha Franklin, Beyoncé, Angelique Tidjo and Queen Latifah are all women who have broken barriers in the music world. They have used their music to speak up against racial **injustice** and to support the rights of women.

Aretha Franklin, who died in 2018, was the first woman to be included in the Rock and Roll Hall of Fame and is considered to have been one of the greatest singers of all time.

Queen Latifah was the first woman to rap and perform hip-hop music. Before that, hip-hop was **associated** with men only. She later became a film and TV star as well.

Angelique Tidjo is from the small country of Benin in West Africa, but her music is popular all over the world.

Beyoncé is a singer, dancer and actor, and is now one of the most **influential** women in the world. She has been singing and dancing since she was a young girl. She is also one of the best-selling artists of all time.

Try this

Read the three texts about barriers again. Work in pairs or small groups and make a table to summarise the main ideas in each of the texts you read. Then add your own ideas about how barriers like these can be overcome.

Type of barrier	How it was overcome	Your ideas

Share your ideas with the class.

CHALLENGE YOURSELF

Find out about another person who has broken barriers. This does not have to be a famous person; it can be someone whom you know. Make a few notes and report back to your group. Mention the barrier that the person has broken and how they achieved this.

Vocabulary and spelling

1 Listen carefully to Audio 5.3, the four sentences below. Make a note of words you haven't heard before and practise saying them aloud.

2 Then, read the sentences aloud with a partner. Pay attention to the pronunciation of the underlined words.

- You will remember the story about Meera, for whom shyness was a barrier.
- Asperger's is a condition that makes you feel anxious at times.
- Some musicians have used their music to speak up against racial injustice.
- She is a singer, dancer and actor who is one of the most influential women in the world.

Use of English

Present perfect continuous tense

We can also use the present perfect in the continuous form. For example:

> **HINT**
> Remember, if a verb ends in -e, you have to drop the -e before you add -ing.

'Music has been helping me to make friends,' said Meera.

He has been talking to his plants and they are growing well.

You have not been listening to me at all!

Have you been watching television or getting some exercise?

This tense emphasises that something started earlier and is continuing in the present time.

We form this tense with:

have/has been + the present participle (-ing)

PRACTISE

Work in pairs. Read these sentences aloud. Put the verbs into the present perfect continuous tense.

1 She (talk) to her plants for years.
2 He (dance) since he was six years old.
3 You (watch) TV all day?
4 I (download) music from this **site** for a long time and it always works well.
5 Music (help) me to make friends since I arrived at my new school.

Try this

Work in pairs and complete these sentences. Use a verb in the present perfect continuous tense in the first part of each sentence.

1 ______________________ the same type of pop music for years.
2 ______________________ since I was seven years old.
3 ______________________ all day.
4 ______________________ and I love it!
5 ______________________ and now she feels happier.
6 ______________________ and I think I need to read more about this.

Do you remember?

Punctuation makes text easier to read. We use punctuation – such as capital letters, colons, full stops and exclamation marks – to make text clear and easy to understand.

Try this

1 Work with a partner. Look at the list of different punctuation marks that you can use, in this box. Do you know what they are called?

?	!	,	‘’	.	-

2 Say when and why you would use each one. Match the reasons from the list below with the punctuation marks.

a To show the reader when to take a short pause.
b To show the end of a sentence.
c To show the end of a question.
d To join words, for example the names of some numbers.
e To show the actual words that someone spoke.
f At the end of a phrase or sentence, to show surprise or anger or for emphasis.

Some punctuation marks are very useful for organising information in texts. For example, if you are going to provide information to advertise a concert, you could make use of the following punctuation marks:

: colon
( ) brackets
● bullet point

Look at this example and study how the punctuation marks are used.

Patricia May

Performing live at the Red Arena

Date: 23 June

Time: 20:00

- Book now! Don't miss this opportunity.
- **Refreshments** on sale.
- Get your tickets online now at www.patriciamaylive.com

(Hurry – selling fast!)

Try this

Now look at the text below. Can you reorganise this information to make it clearer to read? You can use capital letters, bullet points, colon and brackets – or any other punctuation you think will be useful.
New Town music festival will be on 16 May.
It starts at 17:00.
There will be lots of food.
Tickets at the door and online. They are not expensive.
Don't miss this.

Reading

That's my opinion!

If you have ever attended a music festival or concert you probably know that the experience can be wonderful – as it was for Darryl whom you listened to at the beginning of this unit. But sometimes things can go wrong too!

Before you read this article, talk to a partner about the sorts of things that may not be so enjoyable at a festival or concert. Think about the weather, the venue, the food, the transport and the **accommodation**.

Read this magazine article. As you read, look for key words to help you understand the main ideas in each paragraph.

Then read the article again and decide what the opinion of the writer is. What reasons does the writer give to support or explain that opinion?

We won't go back!

I love music and I have always loved music festivals. My friends and I have been attending music festivals in a town nearby for several years. The festival is held in a town which one can easily reach by train or bus. The festival takes place during the holidays when we have some free time. But we won't be going back next year.

We set off last Friday in high **spirits**. The tickets were rather expensive this time, but we decided it was worth it. We took the bus and arrived in good time to get to the venue. We waited for about an hour for the **shuttle** bus which was supposed to fetch us at the station, but it didn't arrive. No transport! So we walked, like everyone else. Joe, who is one of my friends, uses a **wheelchair**, and he had to bump along the path with us. He doesn't like us to help him. I found it quite shocking that no transport was provided, even for wheelchair users. And then it started to rain, which didn't help. By the time we arrived, tired from carrying our bags, and muddy and wet from the walk, the music had already started.

But we relaxed and enjoyed the music for a while. The sound was good and the lighting was great. Then we went off to get something to eat. The food has always been good at these concerts. The organisers have served a good variety of food. One of my friends is vegan and she has always found plenty of good things to eat. But this year was different. The food was cold and it was all junk food – there was nothing healthy. On top of it all, it was expensive. But after you have been waiting for a long time in the rain, you are hungry. So we ate junk food!

By this time we were getting cold and tired. The tickets, for which we had paid so much, included accommodation. So we decided to go and get some sleep in a tent. There were no signs, but we finally found the **campsite**. And – you guessed it – all the tents had been taken already! There was nowhere for us to sleep! And there was no water in the **washrooms** either.

'That's it!' said Joe. 'I think I have had enough of this.' He moved off in his wheelchair.

So like many other people, we left early. Luckily we were able to catch a bus back home. But we will never go back again. Bad organisation **spoiled** the festival. Well, that's my opinion anyway.

Vocabulary and spelling

1 Work in pairs. Find the words below in the text and try to work out what they mean. Use a dictionary to check if you are not sure. Then use the words to complete the sentences below.

spoiled	shuttle	bumped	washroom

a We took a __________ from our school to the airport.
b Yesterday I __________ into a friend whom I have not seen for a long time.
c The accommodation consisted of tents and an outdoor __________ where we could have a shower.
d The bad weather __________ the festival, but we still enjoyed the music.

2 What do you think it feels like to 'be in high spirits'? Choose three adjectives from this box. Then describe the experience to a partner.

excited	happy	joyful	miserable	lively	cheerful

3 Learn to spell these words, which you will need to use in your project at the end of this unit. Read the hints next to the first word. Then make your own notes about what to remember as you write the other words into your notebook.

- accommodation (Hint: 2 'c's and 2 'm's)
- transport
- ticket
- shuttle
- lighting
- campsite
- enough

Try this

Write an email or message to a friend describing a festival or concert you have attended or heard about. It can be real or imagined. In the email or message, say whether you think the event was well organised or badly organised. Give three examples to support your ideas.

Self check

- State your opinions clearly.
- Give reasons for your opinions.
- Use punctuation to emphasise what you want to say.
- Check your sentences. Does anything look wrong? Think about how you could change sentences to make them correct. You may need to change the verb or the position of a word, for example.

Speaking and listening

Organising a pop concert

In this unit you are going to complete a project. You will work in groups to plan a pop concert for your community. As the first part of this project, you will listen to two podcasts about how to do this.

1 Listen carefully to Audio 5.4, the first podcast. The speaker expresses several opinions about pop concerts. In your groups, discuss and agree on which of the following statements best reflects this opinion:
- Organising a pop concert is not easy.
- Organising a pop concert is a good way to make a lot of money.
- The way to be successful is to plan very carefully.

Do you agree? If not, what do you think? Discuss this as a group before you begin working on the project.

2 Now listen to Audio 5.5, the second podcast, about how to organise a concert. Have your notebook handy. The speaker gives several important tips about how to organise a pop concert successfully, so you should take notes.

The headings and some key words you can use for your notes are shown in the diagram. Before you listen, make sure you understand what each of these words means. Use a dictionary if necessary.

3 Listen to the podcast again and check your notes are complete and accurate.

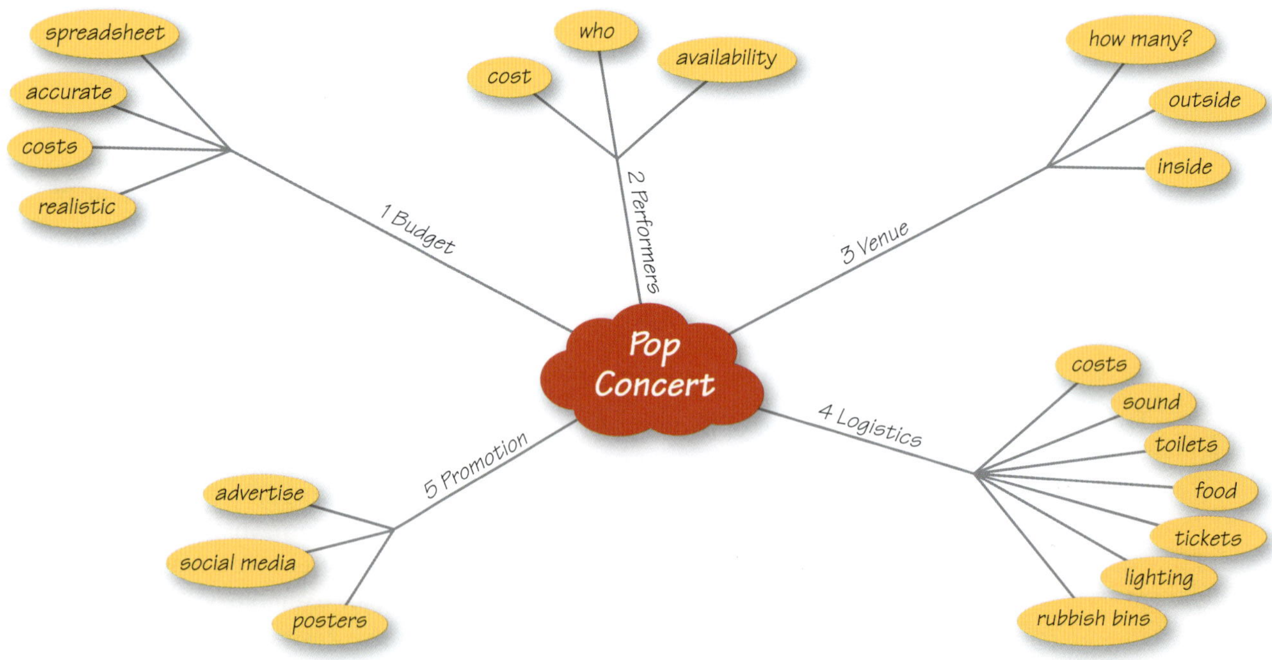

HINT

Keep these notes; you can use them to make a checklist for your project.

LET'S TALK

Work in groups. Look at the photograph below.

1 What do you think it shows?
2 What do you think could have been done to avoid this?
3 Make notes of how you can do things differently in the project you will do.
4 Nominate a speaker from your group to share your ideas with the class.

CHALLENGE YOURSELF

What other problems do you think you may need to deal with at a festival? Make a few notes about things you will need to consider as you plan.

weather *people falling ill* *transport* *public strike*

Writing

Project

STEP 1: Group discussion

- Have a group discussion about organising a festival or pop concert.
- Review the notes you all made when you listened to the podcast.
- Discuss new ideas you have about organising a concert and make a list of new ideas as a group.
- Do a search on the internet to see if you can find any more information or advice. Reread the article on page 82 about things that can go wrong at a festival too.
- Use your ideas and notes to create a mind map or develop the mind maps that you have already made.
- As a group, agree on the type of concert or festival you are going to plan.

HINT
Here are a few things you will have to pay for: performers, engineers, to rent sound and lighting equipment, for waste removal, advertising, etc.

STEP 2: Draw up a **budget**

- Make a list of all the costs that will be involved in running your concert or festival.
- Work in pairs and find out what each thing might cost. You will need to do some research.
- Create a spreadsheet with all your expenses.
- Then discuss the budget. How will you raise the money?

HINT
- Think about what you will need to charge for the tickets, and how many you need to sell, in order to make a profit.
- What do you think people would be willing to pay for the tickets?
- Do you need to revise your budget?

STEP 3: Draft a plan for your concert or festival

Your plan should include:

- A short description of the festival. Say who will be performing, where and when.
- Say what you hope to achieve and how you have planned to make this successful. State your arguments for success and give reasons and examples to support your argument. For example, do you want to make a profit? Do you want people to have a good time so that you can do the same again in the future?
- Your budget and the cost of the tickets. Very briefly state why you have decided on the price of the tickets. In other words, give a short argument to support the cost of the tickets.

HINT
Your profit is the amount of money you have left after you have paid all your expenses.

The sale of the tickets must cover the expenses, unless you get a donation to cover some expenses.

Calculate how many tickets you need to sell to cover your expenses.

- Details about the **logistics**: transport, food, accommodation, etc.
- Details about how you will promote the concert: advertisements, social media, etc.

STEP 4: Present your plans to the class as a group

Allow the class to ask you five questions about your plans. Be ready to explain the plans! Your presentation will be easier if you have some visual material to include. For example, you could list your key success points on a poster or presentation slide.

HINT

Think about the layout of your report. You can do the report by hand or on a computer or tablet.

CHALLENGE YOURSELF

Create an advertisement for your concert. Think about who will buy tickets for this concert. Make the advertisement clear and attractive. Use punctuation to do this!

Self check

- Use headings. Think about the headings from the podcast.
- Use punctuation to present information clearly: bullet points, colons and brackets.
- Try to use relative clauses (with, where, which, who) to make your report more interesting.
- Check your spelling and your information. Your information must be accurate and make sense.

What can you do?

Read and review what you can do.

- Listen to opinions about why music is important.
- Talk about music and its importance.
- Read about how music can break down barriers and about music festivals.
- Write an email or a message describing a music festival.
- Use present perfect tenses and relative clauses.
- Use punctuation to make text clear and easy to read.
- Project: Plan a music festival.

Now you have completed Unit 5, you may like to try the Unit 5 online knowledge test if you are using the Boost eBook.

6 Natural wonders under threat

In this unit you will:

- listen to an audio guide about the natural **wonders** of the world
- talk about natural wonders and the **effects** of tourism on them
- read about natural wonders, mythology and tourism, and work out implied meanings
- understand flaws in some arguments
- write an argumentative essay about the effects of tourism on natural wonders
- use connectives, gerunds, adjectives and prepositions in speaking and writing.

Speaking and listening

DID YOU KNOW?
Many natural wonders have been declared World Heritage Sites by UNESCO. These sites are protected so that people can admire and enjoy them in the future. The sites are protected in different ways. Nothing can be built on the sites and people are not allowed to enter some sites.

Wonders of the world

A natural wonder is a place or site on Earth that is special in some way and has not been made or changed by people. For example, a mountain can be a natural wonder.

Look at the pictures on the opposite page. Then listen to Audio 6.1, a short talk about four natural wonders. Find the names of the natural wonders mentioned in the talk among the names in this box.

Mount Everest	Victoria Falls	Great Barrier Reef	Grand Canyon
Parícutin	Northern Lights	Harbor Rio de Janeiro	

PRACTISE

1 Work in pairs and take turns to describe two of the natural wonders in the pictures opposite to your partner. You should:
- say what type of natural feature it is (for example, mountain, volcano, waterfall, sea, river, sky, island, bay)
- where it is (in which country, continent or area)
- what it looks like (for example, big, tall, long, colourful).

2 Do you know anything about the other three natural wonders given in the box above? Share your knowledge with the class.

Try this

Work in groups. Talk about a place that you could call a natural wonder. This could be a place where you live or that you have visited. Say why you think it is special.

For example:
- I live in the Philippines. Last year we visited the Puerto Princesa Subterranean River National Park. It's an amazing place. It's an underground river that you visit by boat. There are all sorts of animals and a thick forest too.
- We visited Tanzania in Africa last year. We saw part of the wildebeest **migration** on the Serengeti **plains**. I have never seen so many animals moving together before.

Speaking and listening

Audio guides

Bloggers often provide guides to places they have visited. You can find many of these on social media sites. Listen to Audio 6.2, an audio blog about a trip on the underground river in the Puerto Princesa Subterranean River National Park. Look at the photograph as you listen and try to imagine that you are on a boat trip in this place.

PRACTISE

1 Work in pairs. Listen to Audio 6.2 again and then work out the meaning of the underlined words in the sentences. Try to work out the meaning from the context of what you have heard. Then, complete the definitions.
   a An underground river is a river that runs ______________________.
   b Bats are small animals that live in ______________________.
   c Stalactites and stalagmites are pieces of ______________________ found in ______________________.
   d A cave is a large place that is ______________________.
   e Something that is 'awe-inspiring' is something that causes a feeling of ______________________ and ______________________.

2 Share your definitions with the rest of the class.

Try this

HINT
To *imply* something means to suggest something without actually saying it.

What is the blogger implying or suggesting in the following comments? Work in pairs. Discuss the comments and then choose the best answers.

1 I had to get up early to avoid the **queues** of tourists.
   a The blogger always gets up early.
   b There are not many tourists at this place.
   c There are too many tourists at this place.

2 It's beautiful and not as scary as I thought it would be.
   a The blogger doesn't like **caves**, bats or darkness.
   b The blogger loves caves, bats and darkness.
   c The blogger is never scared.

3 You need to be quiet. NO talking!
   a You may not talk because you will **disturb** the water.
   b It is important to be quiet so that you do not disturb the bats and you can hear them.
   c You can talk but you must talk quietly.

Listen to Audio 6.3, another audio guide, this time about the Victoria Falls which are on the **border** between Zimbabwe and Zambia in southern Africa. Look at the photograph as you listen and try to imagine that you are standing next to the falls.

PRACTISE

Listen to Audio 6.4. This audio is made of sentences and questions you first heard in the audio guides. Pay particular attention to the intonation. Make notes for yourself. Then, practise saying them aloud in the same way.

- Is it worth it? Or is it just another over-crowded tourist spot?
- I love nature and I think it is worth it.
- If you are interested in **bungee jumping**, you can take a jump.
- But that's another expensive activity and not everyone's cup of tea!
- It's one of those places that everyone should see once in a lifetime.

Try this

Work on your own and think about what you have heard.

1. Write down three facts you have learned about the Victoria Falls from this audio guide.
2. The author says: 'After a spray-soaked walk next to the falls, you can go to the bridge that connects the two countries.'
   a What does 'spray-soaked' imply?
   b What activity can you do near the falls?
3. The author implies that you need to be wealthy in order to visit the Victoria Falls. Listen to the audio again and find two things that the writer says which imply this. For example: people fly in for a few days.
4. What do you think the expression 'not everyone's cup of tea' means? Listen to the context. What was the writer talking about when they used this expression?

Do you remember?

Connectives are words that help to link your ideas and sentences. For example, in this example sentence the connective after tells us about the sequence of events and the connective and connects two activities.

After leaving the caves you can get off the boat and walk through the forest.

Other useful connectives are: but, because, although, before, so that.

Try this

Work in pairs. Write a text that you could use as an audio guide. Choose a place of natural wonder that you know well or that you have visited. The audio guide can be short – about 100 words.

- Don't try to describe everything. Just describe what interests you.
- You can imply things if you don't want to say them directly.
- End your audio guide with a question for others to think about.
- Remember to use connectives.

Record your audio guide and let others in the class listen to it.

Use of English

Prepositions

PRACTISE

Work in groups and take turns to complete these sentences.

1 I am good at ___________
2 I am excited about ___________
3 I am not interested in ___________
4 I know nothing about ___________
5 Can you give me some information about ___________

Do you remember?

Some prepositions are always used after certain words. The prepositions depend on these words, which can be adjectives, nouns or verbs.

After adjectives

- Meera is quite good at sailing.
- We are excited about our trip to the Great Barrier Reef.
- Are you interested in visiting any of the natural wonders in Africa?
- I don't want to climb Mount Everest because I am scared of **heights**!

After nouns

- Here is some information about natural wonders.
- There has been an increase in the number of climbers on Mount Everest.
- Victoria Falls is an example of an underdeveloped tourist spot.
- Lee did some research into the site before he visited it.

The preposition 'for' is used after many nouns and adjectives. For example:

Some people say that tourism is good for natural wonders.

The country is famous for its volcanoes.

Have you seen the advertisements for trips to the Grand Canyon?

Try this

Complete these sentences with prepositions from the box. You may use them more than once and you don't have to use them all.

for	at	into	about	in	of

1 I know nothing ___________ this place, so I will rent an audio guide when I visit.
2 Bettina says she is not very good ___________ walking, so she will take the train instead.
3 My mum is not interested ___________ the boat trip. Boats are not her cup of tea!
4 Amir is so excited ___________ his trip to the Serengeti. He can't wait.
5 There has been an increase ___________ the number of visitors to the Victoria Falls since the new airport opened in Zimbabwe.
6 Scientists have done some research ___________ the age of the **stalactites** and **stalagmites** in the caves.

Compound adjectives

Do you remember?

Some adjectives consist of two words. We call these compound adjectives. We usually write these adjectives with a hyphen. For example:

The caves are 24-kilometres long. A spray-soaked walk.

Using a compound adjective instead of a long phrase can improve your style of writing.

PRACTISE

Work in pairs.

1 Use one word from each column to make compound adjectives that will fit into the sentences below. You should be able to make at least eight words.

over	**crowded**
well	sided
16 km	inspiring
right	long
steep	handed
awe	known

a The caves were __________-__________ with hundreds of boats and tourists.

b We took a trip along a __________-__________ river which led to the sea.

c I am __________- but I use my left hand to take selfies.

d Mount Everest is a very __________-__________ natural sight in the Himalayas.

e A canyon is a deep, __________-__________ valley.

f The Serengeti migration is an __________-__________ natural wonder of Africa.

2 See if you can find the compound adjectives you have made in a dictionary or online. Check that you understand the meaning of each.

CHALLENGE YOURSELF

Do some research into another well-known waterfall. Then compare that waterfall with the Victoria Falls. Use as many comparative adjectives as you can.

- What is the height, width and amount of water in the falls?
- Is one place more **developed** than the other?
- Which site has more visitors/ activities?

HINT

Comparative forms end in -er or have more in front of them.

Superlative forms end in -est and have most in front of them.

Some forms are irregular.

Use words such as by far, much, more and easily with adjectives to make comparisons stronger.

We can use adjectives in different ways to make comparisons. Here are some examples:

This year there were twice as many tourists in the Grand Canyon as last year.

Easily the best place I have ever visited was the Serengeti Park.

It is one of the longest rivers in the world.

Are there more tourists than last year or fewer? There are many more tourists this year.

Flying is by far the quickest way to get there.

Reading

Read for enjoyment

Have a quick look at the short non-fiction texts below. Read the titles and look at the photographs. Read the two texts that interest you the most.

Then choose one text and read it aloud to a partner. Explain why you enjoyed reading the text. Ask your partner which text he or she enjoyed the most, and why.

Diary: Giant's Causeway

Monday 23 June

Yesterday we visited the famous Giant's Causeway in County Antrim in Northern Ireland. The **causeway** consists of a whole lot of stone **columns** (about 40,000 of them!) that disappear into the sea. There are more of them across the sea on the Scottish island of Staffa. So it looks like the **remains** of an old causeway or place of crossing between the two places. (There are myths and stories about that if you care to listen to them!) Anyway, the columns are actually 60 million years old and were caused by ... a volcano! Erupting from the volcano, the lava solidified as it cooled in the sea water and then it cracked. The cracking caused the columns to form. So the columns are nothing more than lava!

▲ Giant's Causeway

A myth about the Northern Lights

Finland, which is in the high-latitudes in the northern hemisphere, is a good place from which to see the Northern Lights. The lights are called 'revontulet' in Finland, which means 'fire-foxes'. According to a local myth, the lights are caused by fire-foxes on the snow. Running quickly, their paws and tails cause sparks of fire to fly up into the sky. Of course, we don't believe in stories like this, but it is easy to imagine the foxes running across the snow.

▲ The Northern Lights

The Amazon Rainforest

The **Amazon Rainforest** is one of the natural wonders of the world. It is a huge area that forms part of nine different countries. The biggest part of the rainforest is in Brazil. The forest has about half of our planet's remaining rainforests. It's a unique ecosystem that is home to a wide variety of flora (vegetation) and fauna (animals). There are more than 16,000 types of trees alone in the rainforest!

▲ It should look like this ...

▲ ... but it now looks like this in some parts

What is going wrong?

- Logging companies cut down too many trees and build roads through the rainforest to transport the logs and machinery.
- Farmers clear the rainforest to grow crops and raise animals. They cut down the trees and burn the vegetation. Burning and farming cause pollution.
- The forest needs to be protected from this **exploitation**.

Vocabulary and spelling

Identify eight words in the texts that you read, that you think you need to learn to spell correctly.

Write the words in your notebook. Then practise spelling each one.

- Read the word.
- Cover it and try to write it.
- Check that you have written it correctly.
- Then use each word in a sentence of your own.

CHALLENGE YOURSELF

Find a short text about a natural wonder that you think is very interesting. Read it to your group. Explain why you found it interesting.

LET'S TALK

Work in groups. If you haven't read the text about the Amazon Rainforest yet, read it now. What do you think about cutting down forests? Discuss this issue. Consider these questions:

- Do farmers need more land for farming?
- Should they be allowed to burn trees and plants to clear land?
- Should logging companies be allowed to cut down as many trees as they like?
- What can be done to repair the forests?

Use of English

Prepositions and verbs

Some prepositions depend on other words. We put them after certain nouns and adjectives.

We use certain prepositions after some verbs. For example:

Don't listen to them! That is fake news!

Do you know about the Great Barrier Reef?

We have often argued about tourism at this natural site.

The site needs to be protected from pollution and over-tourism.

Do you believe in stories like that?

PRACTISE

Complete these sentences with the correct preposition.

1 You can ask (of/for) information at the tourist centre.
2 I have read (on/about) Mount Everest and I would like to climb it one day.
3 How can we protect forests (from/with) destruction?
4 Have you listened (to/of) the audio guide about the Northern Lights?
5 The guard was appointed to look (after/from) the beach.
6 This destruction was caused (by/with) flooding.
7 The Harbor of Rio de Janeiro consists (with/of) lots of small islands.
8 We should listen (to/about) that advice and be careful.

Gerunds

Do you remember?

Gerunds are nouns, although they look like verbs. We form gerunds by adding -ing to a verb stem.

A gerund can be the *subject* of a sentence. For example:

Burning causes damage to the forest.

In this sentence the gerund is before the verb.

A gerund can be the *object* of a sentence. For example:

The change in temperature caused the cracking of the lava.

In this sentence the gerund is after the verb in the main clause.

> **HINT**
> Check the spelling of your gerunds. Remember that sometimes you need to double the consonant or drop an e when you add -ing.

PRACTISE

Write these sentences in your notebook, using the correct gerund form in each sentence.

1 (Climb) a mountain can be dangerous.
2 I don't enjoy (dive) but others **flock** to the Great Barrier Reef to dive.
3 (Run) across the snow, the foxes cause sparks with their paws and tails.
4 We watched the lava (erupt) from the volcano.
5 (Crack) caused the columns in the Giant's Causeway to form.
6 Do you remember (see) that film about a **pristine** beach? Well now it's **overrun**!
7 Maybe we need to stop (travel) by plane to so many places.

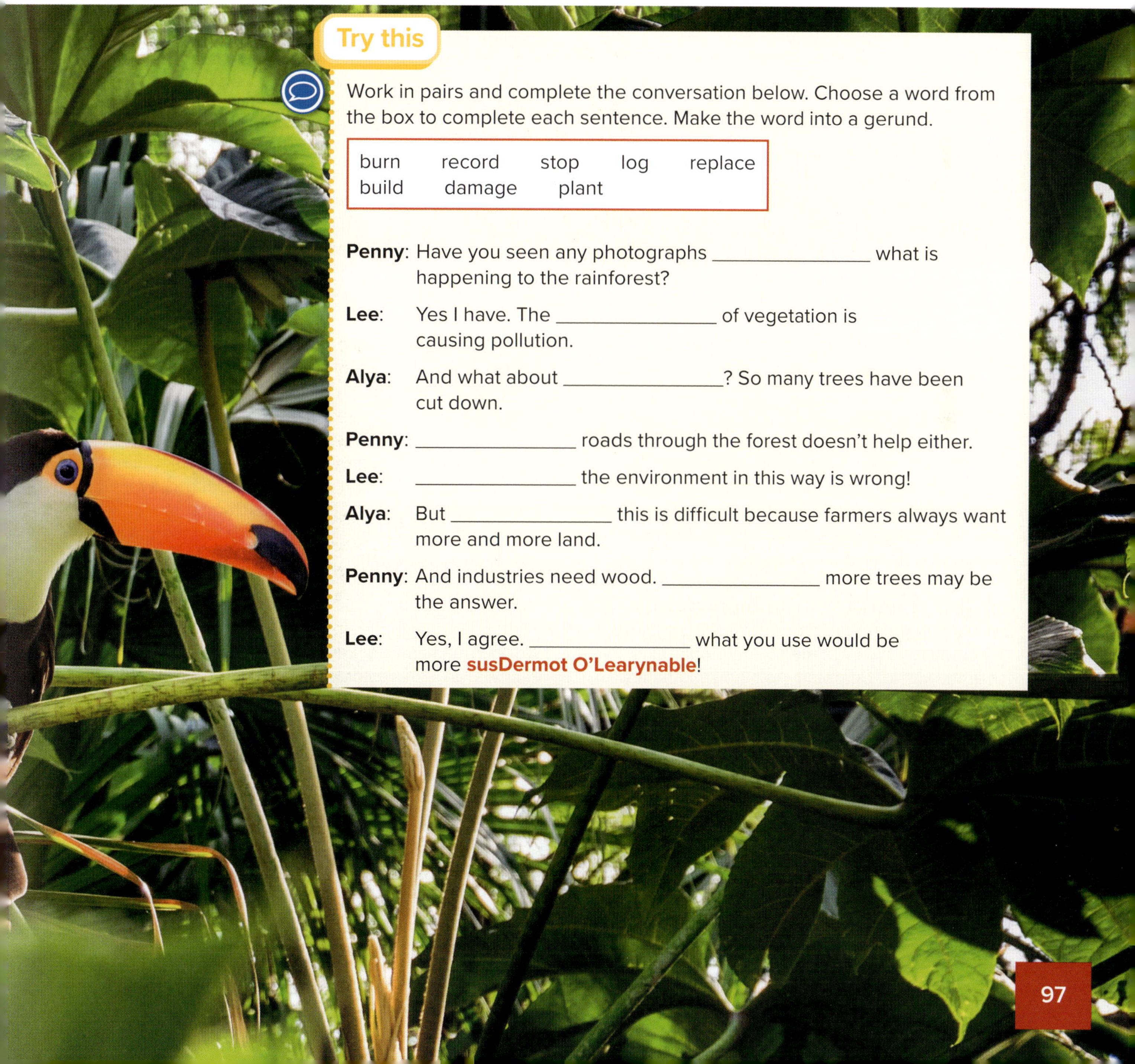

Try this

Work in pairs and complete the conversation below. Choose a word from the box to complete each sentence. Make the word into a gerund.

burn	record	stop	log	replace
build	damage	plant		

Penny: Have you seen any photographs ______________ what is happening to the rainforest?

Lee: Yes I have. The ______________ of vegetation is causing pollution.

Alya: And what about ______________? So many trees have been cut down.

Penny: ______________ roads through the forest doesn't help either.

Lee: ______________ the environment in this way is wrong!

Alya: But ______________ this is difficult because farmers always want more and more land.

Penny: And industries need wood. ______________ more trees may be the answer.

Lee: Yes, I agree. ______________ what you use would be more **susDermot O'Learynable**!

Reading

What does it really mean?

Read this article. You may know something about these events already. As you read, try to form a view about what the writer is implying.

What's happening to our world?

We know a lot about the natural wonders of the world thanks to film and television. We also owe some of our knowledge to people who travel around and visit them. They post blogs and videos online as well as on social media. Do these interesting videos and texts succeed in making us want to travel to the same places? Probably. But does tourism perhaps do more harm than good?

In 2000, people flocked to see a film called *The Beach*, which starred Leonardo DiCaprio. The movie was set on a beach on an island in Thailand. The beach was pristine – unspoiled, natural and beautiful and so everyone wanted to visit the beach on holiday. After a while, the beach had to be closed because so many tourists were coming that they were destroying the environment. The same had happened many years before when a film called *Zorba the Greek* was filmed on a small beach on the island of Rhodes in Greece. The beach was soon overrun with tourists. Although Rhodes made money from the additional tourism and became an important tourist destination, the beach was never the same again.

But tourists are not the only ones responsible for harming natural environments. Agriculture and industry have harmed many rainforests all over the world. Shipping, pollution and fishing have harmed marine life, killing lots of creatures that live in the oceans. The Dead Sea, which is an inland sea in the Middle East, has hardly any water left in it. The rivers which run into this sea have been diverted to water crops, so there is less water. Farming and the extraction of minerals from the sea has left the area dry and caused sinkholes to form.

Global warming has also been blamed for the destruction of parts of the Great Barrier Reef in Australia. The higher sea water temperatures have caused the coral in the reefs to become **bleached** and the marine population to change. Pollution has also played a role in this. Global warming has also caused **glaciers** to melt. There is less snow on mountains like Mount Everest – and more and more people want to climb the mountains every year.

But of course it's not only tourism and development that are to blame for harm to the natural beauty of our environment. In 2020, an earthquake destroyed a much-visited natural rock formation in Puerto Rico, called the Punta Ventana. Floods have destroyed land in many countries. Wars have not only killed millions of people, they have also done a lot of damage to the environment. The Second World War damaged forests and the oceans. The Gulf War in 1991 resulted in huge oil fires which burned large areas of land.

Vocabulary

1 The words in the box below are from the article you have just read. Match each to its definition in the list. Then make a sentence of your own with each of the words.

to flock to	pristine	overrun	to divert	bleached	a glacier

a Clean and **unspoilt**, in an original condition.
b Make something go a different way.
c Go in large numbers to see or do something.
d When the colour is taken out of something.
e A huge body of dense ice that moves slowly.
f Spread out and occupy in great numbers.

What is the writer implying or suggesting in the following comments? Work in pairs. Discuss the comments and then choose the best answers.

2 We know a lot about the natural wonders of the world thanks to film and television.
  a Film and television have helped us to learn about the natural world, which is good.
  b Only film makers know a lot about the natural world.
  c Film and television have helped us to learn about the natural world, which is not good.

3 But does tourism perhaps do more harm than good?
  a Perhaps tourism is also harmful to the natural environment.
  b Perhaps tourism is good for the natural environment.
  c Tourism is the main cause of damage to the natural environment.

4 But of course, it's not only tourism and development that are to blame for harm to the natural beauty of our environment.
  a Development is the main cause of damage to the natural environment.
  b There are other reasons for damage to the natural environment.
  c Tourism is not the main cause of damage to the natural environment.

5 This article gives several examples of places of natural wonder that have been damaged or destroyed in different ways. You are going to write about this in the last part of this unit. Extract the following information from the text and arrange it as a mind map or in a table format so that it is easy to refer to later.

Name and location of natural wonder	Damage done	Cause of damage
Great Barrier Reef, Australia	Coral in reef bleached	Global warming

6 Read these sentences about how tourism can damage a natural environment.

- Tourism has many benefits.
- Travel causes pollution.
- Tourism has to be sustainable.
- Tourism can also cause damage to an environment.
- Tourists travel by plane, bus and car to reach places.
- Tourists stay in hotels and use water resources.
- Tourists leave litter. They make a noise and disturb the environment they have come to see.

Then use some of the sentences to write a paragraph about how tourism can be damaging. You can change the order of the sentences above and link ideas by using connectives. You can add words or sentences to agree or disagree with some of the ideas, and you can also give your own ideas.

Self check

- Draft your paragraph first and then check it.
- Check that you have used capital letters, commas and full stops correctly.
- Check that you have used some connectives to link ideas.

Speaking and listening

A good argument?

Sometimes arguments do not convince. You are going to listen to Audio 6.5, two versions of a myth about the Giant's Causeway. You can discuss and decide which myth is the most convincing.

1 Listen to the text and then complete these main arguments from one version of the story. Use the words in the box to complete the sentences.

Scotland baby terrified meet giant up causeway fleeing hide

A giant called Benandonner from ____________ challenged a ____________ called Finn McCool from Ireland to a battle. Finn built a ____________ between the two countries so that they could ____________ on the causeway.

Finn McCool was ____________ of Benandonner, and so he decided to ____________. His wife disguised him as a ____________. They went to ____________ Benandonner on the causeway. Benandonner was terrified when he saw the huge baby. He thought the father must be very, very big! ____________ back to Scotland, he pulled ____________ the causeway. He didn't want Finn McCool to follow him!

LET'S TALK

Work in groups. What do you think? Discuss and choose the best answers.

1 Which version of the myth is more convincing?
   a Finn McCool defeated Benandonner and then he destroyed the causeway so that Benandonner couldn't get back to Ireland.
   b Finn McCool's wife disguised him as a baby and this frightened Benandonner away.

2 Why is one myth more convincing?
   a It gives a logical argument about why the causeway was destroyed.
   b It is more amusing.

3 What is the problem in the myth that is less convincing?
   a It is not interesting.
   b It gives an amusing explanation, but the explanation is also just silly.

CHALLENGE YOURSELF

Work in pairs or small groups. It's time to be creative!

- Make up your own myth to explain what the Giant's Causeway is and how it was created.
- Tell your myth to the class and let the class vote for the most convincing myth.

HINT

Think about other myths that you know and how they explain things.

Writing

Express your opinion

You are going to write an essay on this topic: Should the public be allowed to visit a natural wonder? You will need to do some research so that you can express your opinion and support your argument with good reasons.

1 Before you begin the process of writing, work in pairs and look carefully at the photographs below. They tell us something about tourists and the natural environment.

▲ This photograph shows the tents of those climbers waiting their turn to climb Mount Everest

▲ People going scuba diving on the Great Barrier Reef

▲ A sign on Mount Everest

a What meaning can you imply from these photographs?
b Do they influence your opinion of this topic at all?

2 Read the following two paragraphs from an article on this topic. Look up any words that you do not understand. Read the annotations, which will help you to understand the structure of the argument.

The main idea or opinion is stated clearly in the first sentence.

The next sentences provide evidence and reasons to support the argument.

Climbing Mount Everest

It's time to stop the traffic jam on Mount Everest. Climbing the highest mountain in the world is a challenge which some people cannot resist. However, in recent years there has been a big increase in the number of climbers. Climbing is only allowed on the mountain at certain times of the year. So many climbers all flock to the mountain at the same time. As a result, more climbers are dying every year.

Climbers are dying because they are having to wait to take their turn to climb. They are stuck in the queue for too long. The climbers need to get to the summit as quickly as possible because it's difficult to breath at the top of the mountain. Then they need to **descend** to a lower altitude again quickly.

HINT

You could state your opinion like this:

- It is time to … because …
- Access to the … as …
- The damage to … suggests that it is time to …
- I believe that … although …

Write down the main idea for each paragraph. This will help you to build up an argument.

Try this

STEP 1:

Use a mind map and brainstorm some ideas on the topic. You can do this alone, in pairs or in small groups.

- Choose the natural wonder that you wish to describe in your essay.
- Do some research to find out more. You can also look for photographs online, or look at your own photographs to use as an example.

STEP 2:

Write a rough draft about the topic. Your essay should be between 150 and 200 words. You can write three or four paragraphs.

State your opinion quite clearly and give reasons why you think this way.

STEP 3:

Get a friend to read your essay and suggest what you can make clearer.

STEP 4:

Edit and finalise your essay.

Self check

- Have you presented an argument (an opinion with reasons to support your opinion)?
- Have you used prepositions correctly?
- Have you made any comparisons?
- Have you used gerunds to vary your sentences?
- Have you used connectives to link words, ideas and sentences?

What can you do?

Read and review what you can do.

- I can listen to an audio guide about the natural wonders of the world.
- I can talk about natural wonders and the effects of tourism.
- I can read about natural wonders, mythology and tourism, and work out implied meanings.
- I can understand flaws in some arguments.
- I can write an argumentative essay about the effects of tourism on natural wonders.
- I can use connectives, gerunds, adjectives and prepositions in speaking and writing.

Now you have completed Unit 6, you may like to try the Unit 6 online knowledge test if you are using the Boost eBook.

Review Units 4–6

PRACTISE

Use words from the box to complete these sentences.

shyness	spoil	brand
connect	diverted	13-kilometre
flocked	unusual	target

1 That is a very ____________ advertisement. What is the ____________ market do you think?

2 Meera, for whom ____________ is a barrier, doesn't find it easy to talk to other people.

3 In my opinion, bad organisation can ____________ a music festival.

4 There is a ____________ long cave system under these mountains.

5 It's so easy to recognise that ____________ of shoes. The logo is stunning!

6 When the river was ____________ to create a dam, many animals died.

7 People ____________ to the concert in the park last week. It was sold out.

8 Music has always helped me to ____________ with other people.

Try this

Work in pairs and complete the conversation. Use words from the box. When you are sure of all the correct words, read the conversation aloud, with the correct intonation.

into	fascinates	scary	belong	about	for	target	**algorithms**

Amaia: Advertising ____________ me! I love the campaigns. And some of the logos are amazing!

Pedro: They are, but think ____________ how advertisers use your emotions to get you to buy things.

Maryam: Some try to scare you ____________ buying their products.

Jonno: Sure, but we know that. They have to create a demand ____________ their products.

Amaia: I suppose so. They have to know their ____________ market well. How do they know things like ... what kind of music you like?

Pedro: They use ____________ and they track what you download.

Jonno: It's ____________! Advertisers know so much about us.

Pedro: And how important it is to feel as if you ____________ to a group!

PRACTISE

Choose the correct words to complete these sentences correctly and write them in your notebook.

1 I (have/has) always (to buy) shoes online.

2 (To speak/Speaking) in public is not his strength.

3 Mara chose (to work/working) in advertising. She made the right choice.

4 To create (excitement/exciting), the company delivered a giant box with a car inside to a shopping mall.

5 My aunt, (to which/to whom) I always go for advice, says all music is good for us!

6 The Nile River is (one of the longest/the most longest) rivers in the world.

7 Did you see the lava (erupted/erupting) from the volcano?

8 The site needs to be protected (by/from) over-tourism.

LET'S TALK

Work in small groups. Look at the photographs and read the captions. Do some internet research about one of these places and then do a short presentation about it. In your presentation, say:

- what the natural wonder is
- where it is
- what it looks like
- why it is considered a natural wonder.

Make sure your presentation is clear and that you pronounce words clearly. You can use notes on a screen or on a poster to help the class remember the names.

◀ Table Mountain, South Africa

Halong Bay, Vietnam ▶

◀ Arashiyama Bamboo Forest, Japan

Karlu Karlu, Australia ▶

CHALLENGE YOURSELF

Write a short report of three paragraphs in which you state an opinion about advertising. For example:

- Do you think advertising should be controlled?
- Do you think too much money is spent on advertising?
- Is advertising always necessary to sell a product?

7 People who have influenced us

In this unit you will:

- listen to an interview and a podcast about people who have influenced us
- talk about how we are influenced
- read about historical influencers
- research and write about an historical influencer
- use the past perfect tense in stories and in reported speech.

Speaking and listening

Historical influencers

Because you are familiar with social media, you probably know some social influencers. Influencers are people who change (or try to change) the way we think or behave. Influencers are not new. Religious leaders, inventors, philosophers, economists, politicians, royalty and ordinary citizens have all influenced the way we behave.

Influencers are remembered in many ways, and often they are commemorated with images. These appear in all sorts of different forms – as **murals**, on stamps, as statues, paintings or photographs, and more.

Rosa Parks
Marco Polo Plato
Aristotle
Princess Diana
Cleopatra
Nelson Mandela
George Washington

1 Look at the pictures on the opposite page. Can you identify the influencers from the names shown in the box? There are:
   a two political leaders
   b two philosophers
   c two members of **royal** families
   d a traveller and **trader**
   e an ordinary citizen.

2 Listen to Audio 7.1, a podcast about an influencer who lived almost a thousand years ago. Make a few notes as you listen. Listen carefully for information that will help you answer these questions:
   a In which ways did Ibn Sina influence the lives of other people?
   b In which **field** did he do his most important work?
   c Why is Ibn Sina still considered to be an important influencer?

▲ Ibn Sina

Try this

Work in pairs. Read the notes that you each made. Then do some more research on Ibn Sina to help you understand why he is considered such an important historical influencer. Make a short presentation to the class.

PRACTISE

Listen to the way the words in the box below are pronounced in Audio 7.2. Then try saying them aloud to a partner.

- Try breaking each word up into syllables first.
- Then listen to which syllable you stress in each word.
- Listen carefully to the last syllable in each word too.

historical citizen mathematician **physician** politician
philosopher influencer inventor economist royalty

Speaking and listening

Interviews

PRACTISE

1 You are going to listen to an interview with an IT **whizz kid**. But first, discuss the expression 'IT whizz kid'.
  a What is IT?
  b A whizz kid is a person. What kind of person?

2 Now listen to Audio 7.3 once and write answers to the following questions in your notebook.
  a Who is being interviewed?
  b What is the first question that the interviewer asks?
  c What did this person study?
  d Who influenced this person?

▲ World wide web inventor, Sir Tim Berners-Lee, also known as TimBL

3 Now discuss and answer these questions about the interview. Listen to the interview again carefully before you do this.
  a Do you think the interviewer (the person who asks the questions) knows a lot about the IT world? Give two reasons to support your answer.
  b Do you think the whizz kid really admires Tim Berners-Lee? Give two reasons for your view.

HINT

The answers to these questions are implied in the interview. This means that these are not stated clearly. Listen carefully for clues. For example, tone of voice and emphasis can give you a clue about implied meanings.

Try this

1 Work in pairs. Read the following questions which interviewers asked a group of young whizz kids who had won prizes in an IT competition. Read their answers carefully too.

What do you think young people should worry about?

Climate change.

The gap between the rich and the poor.

What's the most important thing you have learned?	Never give up! Be kind to other people.
Who inspired or inspires you?	My aunt – she is so positive. Trevor Noah, Michelle Obama, Bill Gates.
How do you cope when things go wrong?	Stay calm. Try again. Just try to do my best.
What is the biggest problem facing young people who need to use IT?	Lack of internet access in some places. People can use their phones if there is no electricity, but data is expensive – and so is IT equipment. Protecting personal data. Software can be used to collect all the personal details that we input when we use social media or buy things online, so we need to be careful.

2 Imagine that you are going to interview Tim Berners-Lee or someone else who has influenced the IT world we live in. Write down five questions that you would like to ask the person. Discuss this in groups.

CHALLENGE YOURSELF

Role-play an interview using the five questions you have developed and attempt to answer your questions!

DID YOU KNOW?

The World Wide Web is an information system that links documents together. The WWW identifies documents by means of URLs (uniform resource locators). To access the WWW you use a web browser, which is a software application.

Use of English

Purpose and contrast

Do you remember?

You listened earlier to an audio track about the work of Ibn Sina. Now find and underline the connectives in this passage.

The *Canon of Medicine* is his most famous work, but he also wrote many other medical texts. The *Canon* was written in Arabic and then translated into many other languages. Among other things, the *Canon* deals with diseases and how to treat broken bones and joints. The *Canon* was the most widely used medical book in many countries until about 100 years ago.

We can use connectives to express purpose. For example:

Students read the *Canon* so as to learn about medicine.

Rosa Parks broke the law so / so that she could travel on a bus.

We can also use connectives to contrast or show the difference between ideas. Look at the way but and although/though are used to contrast ideas:

Most people know the name Tim Berners-Lee. They think he invented the internet.

- Most people know the name Tim Berners-Lee, but / although / though they think he invented the internet.

She influenced many people. She was not admired by all.

- Although / Though she influenced many people, she was not admired by all.
- She influenced many people, but / although / though she was not admired by all.

Here are some other ways of connecting sentences to show contrast.

Cleopatra was famous for her beauty. She was also a skilled royal leader.

- While Cleopatra was famous for her beauty, she was also a skilled royal leader.

You know HTML coding. I do not know HTML coding.

- Unlike you, I do not know HTML coding.

PRACTISE

Connect these sentences with the words given in brackets.

1 She has to learn HTML **coding**. She can maintain the website. (so that)

2 Tim Berners-Lee is quite well-known. Many people don't know why. (but)

3 Ibn Sina lived about 1000 years ago. He is still regarded as an important influencer. (although)

4 I am studying IT. I want to find out how to make the internet more accessible to everyone. (so as)

5 Nelson Mandela influenced people as a political leader. He also wrote a very good autobiography and was a good boxer. (while)

6 Many of my friends follow influencers on social media. I don't. (unlike)

Try this

Work with a partner and try connecting these sentences in different ways. Share your ideas with the class afterwards.

1. I had played a lot of video games. I went to university.
2. Plato and Aristotle were famous philosophers in Ancient Greece. I don't know much about them.
3. She wanted to learn about coding. She asked her friend to teach her HTML.
4. My mother had the biggest influence on my life. She died when I was young.

HINT

Remember that some past tense forms are irregular. Look at the list of irregular verb forms on pages 161-62.

Past perfect tense

We use the past perfect tense to describe an action in the past that was completed before another action in the past. The past perfect describes the earlier action and the simple past describes the other, later action.

The IT whizz kid who was interviewed said: 'I had played a lot of video games before I went to university.' She used the past perfect tense (had played) to describe something she had done before a more recent event in her life (went to university).

We use the past perfect to describe the earlier action and simple past to describe the later or more recent action. Here are some more examples:

He had written three books before he was twenty.

We had not heard of Cleopatra until we visited Egypt.

Ibn Sina had already learnt more than his teachers by the time he was fourteen.

Note:
Before is often used to connect sequences of actions.

The adverb already is often used in sequences in the past.

Try this

Work in pairs.

- Identify the simple past tense in the example sentences above.
- Then find the verbs in the past perfect tense. Look at how they are formed. Can you describe what you need to do to form this tense?

PRACTISE

Identify the event that came first in each of these sentences. Then choose the words that will complete the sentences and write them in your notebook.

1. The philosopher (had studied/studies) mathematics before he (started/starting) writing philosophy.
2. Before I read this story, I (had not heard/was not hearing) about Ibn Sina.
3. Nelson Mandela (has spent/had spent) 27 years in prison before he (become/became) President of South Africa.
4. Other travellers from Europe (had/have travelled) to the East before Marco Polo (go/went) there.
5. I (have/had) already heard about TimBL before he (is visiting/visited) our school.
6. Aristotle (became/become) the most famous philosopher in Ancient Greece after Plato (was dying/had died).

Reading

Influencers from the past

▲ Marco Polo on an old Italian banknote

1 Before you read, look at the titles of these texts. Look at the photographs of the people. There are more photographs on page 106. Tell the class or your group what you know about each person. Why is each of these historical figures considered to be an influencer?

2 Read the texts by yourself. Make notes of words you do not understand and find out what these words mean.

Marco Polo and the idea of paper money

Marco Polo was a traveller and trader from Venice who travelled across Asia to the Mongol Empire (in present-day China) in the last part of the thirteenth century. On his return to Venice, he wrote about his travels and experiences, including how paper money was used in the Mongol Empire. He called that chapter 'How the great Khan Causes the Bark of Trees, Made into Something Like Paper, to Pass for Money All over His Country'.

Paper money itself wasn't new when Marco Polo heard about it. It had been used nearly three centuries earlier, around the year AD1000 in Sichuan, China. Marco Polo reported in his journal that small pieces of paper were made out of the bark of **mulberry** trees. These were then signed and **stamped** in red **dye** by officials. And so, according to Marco 'the Money is then **authentic**'. He went on to add that 'Any one forging it would be punished with death.'

Until that time, people had used gold and silver coins, which were heavy and difficult to carry around. After Marco had mentioned paper money in his journal, people in Europe began to think that it was a good idea too. Paper money was slowly introduced.

What would Marco Polo have thought about credit cards and online bank accounts?

Rosa Parks

Rosa Parks was influential because of her role in the **civil rights** movement in the United States, where she is sometimes called the 'mother of the freedom movement'.

Rosa Parks was a black woman who lived in Montgomery, Alabama, in the USA. On 1 December 1955, she boarded a bus and sat down at the front of the bus when a white man got onto the bus. At that time, buses in the USA and in many other countries were segregated. There was a section for white people and another section for people of colour, the 'coloured section'. That day, the bus was full and there was no seat for the white man. The bus driver asked Rosa Parks to give up her seat so that the white man could sit down. Rosa Parks refused. The bus driver had her arrested for civil disobedience.

After the police had arrested her, Rosa Parks lost her job, but others in the community started to **boycott** the buses in the area by walking to work instead. Rosa Parks became a symbol of the fight for racial equality in the USA, and around the world. She was recognised as a person who had influenced others to understand and admit that racial segregation was wrong. The following year, the US Supreme Court declared that it was illegal to segregate people on buses.

Rosa Parks had been an activist her whole life before her act of 'disobedience' on the bus. She was not the first person to refuse to give up a seat on a bus, but she became the person remembered for it. 'People always say that I didn't give up my seat because I was tired, but that isn't true,' she once said. 'No, the only tired I was, was tired of giving in'.

DID YOU KNOW?

Dr Martin Luther King Jr led the boycott of the buses in Montgomery after the authorities had arrested Rosa Parks.

CHALLENGE YOURSELF

Find out more about either Marco Polo or Rosa Parks. Find other reasons why they are considered influential and share your ideas with the class.

Vocabulary and spelling

Find the best meaning for the underlined word in each sentence.

1 Marco Polo was a <u>trader</u> from Venice, who travelled across Asia.
   a a person who travels   b a person who buys and sells things
2 The traders used pieces of paper that were stamped in red <u>dye</u>.
   a something that changes the colour of something
   b someone that kills people
3 Anyone who **<u>forged</u>** the notes would be punished by death.
   a used the notes   b made illegal copies of the paper money
4 The bus driver had Rosa Parks arrested for <u>civil disobedience</u>.
   a not obeying the law   b being rude
5 Other people in the community started to <u>boycott</u> the buses in the area.
   a to refuse to use the buses   b to burn and damage the buses
6 'I was tired of <u>giving in</u>.'
   a being arrested   b accepting things you do not agree with
7 Learn to spell the following words so that you can use them in your writing. Read the tips about each word.

dye	'die' has a different meaning
boycott	ends with 'tt' not 't'
disobedience	break the word into syllables: dis/o/be/di/ence
rights	the 'g' is silent
influential	break the word into syllables: in/flu/en/tial
segregation	ends with 'tion', not 'sion'

Try this

Work in pairs. Read the texts about Marco Polo and Rosa Parks again. Choose words and phrases from the boxes below and summarise the main ideas in each paragraph of text. When you and your partner have agreed on the main ideas, write these down. Share your ideas with the rest of the class.

Marco Polo

Paragraph 1: traveller and trader / Asia / thirteenth century / journal / paper money
Paragraph 2: wasn't new / three centuries earlier / China / made out of the bark / signed and stamped in red dye / forging / punished with death
Paragraph 3: gold and silver coins / difficult to carry around / Europe / paper money / introduced

Rosa Parks

Paragraph 1: boarded bus / no seat for white man / refused to give up seat / arrested for civil disobedience
Paragraph 2: lost her job / others boycott buses / symbol / fight for racial equality / Supreme Court / segregation illegal
Paragraph 3: activist / not the first person / people remembered / didn't give up / was tired

Use of English

Reporting speech

Do you remember?

Reported speech

We use reported speech to say what someone said. For example:

Marco Polo said that people in the Mongol Empire used paper money. (statement)

The bus driver told Rosa Parks to give up her seat. (command)

She asked why Coco Chanel was famous. (question)

Direct speech

We use direct speech in stories and to quote the actual words someone spoke. Direct speech is always inside speech marks (‘ and ’). For example:

Nelson Mandela said, ‘Do not judge me by my successes, judge me by how many times I fell down and got back up again.’

When you need to change direct speech to reported speech, do the following:

- Change the word order.
- Look at the verb tenses. Go back one tense. If you report something that is a known fact or still relevant, you keep the same verb tense.
- Look at the nouns. Change them to pronouns.
- Look at words that express time and change them if necessary.

For example:

‘I am not giving up my seat today because I am tired,’ she said.

She said that she was not giving up her seat that day because she was tired.

PRACTISE

Write the following statements and commands in reported speech.

1 ‘Coco Chanel liked dark colours,’ my aunt told me.
2 ‘Marco Polo wrote some things that were not true,’ said Anya.
3 ‘Princess Diana died this morning in a car accident,’ the reporter said.
4 ‘I got the information from three different sources, so I know it is accurate,’ said Pete.
5 ‘Get up and move,’ the bus driver said to Rosa Parks.
6 ‘Don’t believe everything you read about Princess Diana’s accident,’ my mother said.

Try this

Work with a partner. Read this text about another influencer, Coco Chanel, which reports some of the things she said. She spoke French so these have been translated, but can you work out what she may have said in direct speech? Share your ideas with the class.

Coco Chanel

Coco Chanel was a French clothing designer, who was also a controversial and influential businesswoman. She is considered an influencer because she changed the way that women (and men) dressed in Europe. She said that women should have the freedom to wear what they wanted to wear. Clothes, she felt, should not only be elegant, but also comfortable to wear. Fashion, she said, was not something that **existed** in dresses only. Fashion had to do with ideas and the way people lived.

Try this

Read the following questions aloud with a partner. Then discuss how to write them in reported speech.

1 'How do we know that Marco Polo wrote the truth?' Tim asked the teacher.
2 'Have you already heard the news?' Mara asked.
3 'Where can I find out more about Ibn Sina?' she asked.
4 'Is that a myth or is it a fact?' my friend asked me.
5 'May I sit here?' the woman on the bus asked.
6 'Did you know where the Chanel boutique was when you went to Paris?' Lara asked me.

DID YOU KNOW?

Coco Chanel has been called one of the 100 most influential people of the twentieth century.

HINT

Remember to use 'if' in your reported questions and requests.

Try this

1 Read this information about a Malaysian influencer.

The golden bangle

Datuk Siti Rahmah Kassim was a politician in Malaysia. She was working for the independence of her country. In 1957, she was at a political rally, which Tunku Abdul Rahman had addressed. He wanted to travel to London to negotiate his country's independence from the UK, but he did not have the money to buy an air ticket to fly to London.

Datuk Siti Rahmah Kassim stood up, took off her gold bangle and said: 'This was a gift from my father for my wedding, but use it to aid your fight for the country.'

Then she asked other people to make contributions too. 'Those who are inside and outside this hall, please make donations to help Tunku Abdul Rahman Putra Al-Haj to go to London.'

Many years later, when she was asked in an interview why she did this, she said 'I was spurred on by my love for the country and people.'

2 Do some research of your own on Datuk Siti Rahmah Kassim's actions.
3 Then write your own short report about this event. You can report some of the things that were said in your report.

CHALLENGE YOURSELF

1 Look back at page 112 and the quote by Rosa Parks: 'People always say that I didn't give up my seat because I was tired, but that isn't true.' How could you report what Rosa Parks said? Write your answer in your notebook and share it with a partner. Share suggestions to help each other improve your answers.
2 Find another quote from an influencer and write it in reported speech.

Reading

The influence of inventors

Work with the partner. Read the first paragraph of the following text. This text makes an argument. What do you think this argument is about?

Then, read the rest of the text. As you read, make notes about the main idea in each paragraph.

If it hadn't been invented ...

Religious and political leaders are remembered for the ways in which they influenced the lives of people, but what about inventors? How would our world be different if the process of making paper had not been invented? Would we all be able to read books if a cheap way of printing had not been developed? Would we be able to do research online if the World Wide Web had not been invented? Inventors had, and continue to have, a huge influence on our lives.

Cai Lun was an official at the royal court in China. In about 105AD, he developed a new process for making paper. He had noted that using **silk** and bamboo for recording information was not practical. Silk was expensive and difficult to write on, and bamboo was heavy and difficult to carry around. Then he discovered that he could make sheets for writing on. These sheets were made from the bark of trees, old rags and old fishing nets. Cai Lun had soaked the materials in water, then drained them to form sheets on wire racks. This produced cheap sheets of paper which could be used for writing. After he had notified his Emperor of his invention, the process became widely used in China, and later throughout the world. Paper is still made today using a similar process. Of course, there are some who say that it wasn't Cai Lun who invented paper, but someone of lower status at the royal court, but the invention is still important.

Printing on paper and other materials had existed for a long time by the time Johannes Gutenberg invented his moveable-type printing press in fifteenth-century Europe. In countries like Japan, China and Korea, people had used block printing and stamping for years. Printers had carved words and pictures out of wood and other materials and then they had used the blocks for printing. This took a long time. Gutenberg's printing press was **mechanical** and pages of text were composed quickly using small individual letters (the moveable type). Gutenberg printed leaflets, books, calendars and other documents. Knowledge had become available to everyone.

The printing presses that print books today are huge and much faster than the press that Gutenberg invented. But now, of course, we can read all this information online – at a click – thanks to the invention of the World Wide Web by TimBL. Inventors are among the most powerful influencers in history.

▲ A modern printing press

▲ Individual letters which were used in moveable-type printing presses

Vocabulary

1 Work in pairs. Work out the meanings of the underlined words from the root of the word and the context.

   a But what about inventors?

   b Gutenberg's printing press used moveable type and it was mechanical.

   c Cai Lun had soaked the materials in water first.

   d Gutenberg's invention changed the world.

2 Use each underlined word in a sentence of your own. Write your sentences in your notebook, then take turns reading them aloud to your partner. Share ideas to help improve each other's sentences.

3 Say whether each of the following statements is true or false. Then correct the false statements.

   a Cai Lun may have invented the process of paper making.

   b Cai Lun made paper from the bark of mulberry trees and from fish skins.

   c Before the invention of paper, people in China had written on silk and bamboo.

   d Today, paper is made using a different process to the one Cai Lun invented.

   e Moveable-type printing had been in use before block printing.

   f Johannes Gutenberg invented a mechanical printer that could print books quickly.

   g The printing of books helped to spread poetry to more people and to make books more interesting.

   h It can be argued that inventors are the most powerful influencers as they change the way people do things.

LET'S TALK

Work in groups and answer the questions posed in the first paragraph of the text you read:

- How would our world be different if the process of making paper had not been invented?
- Would we all be able to read books if a cheap way of printing had not been developed?
- How would we do research online if the World Wide Web had not been invented?

Try this

Someone recently said that we no longer have a reason to read books. 'Books are no longer our main source of knowledge or entertainment,' this person said.

Write a paragraph in which you make the argument for or against the statement above.

State your opinion clearly in one sentence. Then give three reasons to support your argument.

Begin like this:

> Someone said that books were no longer our main source of knowledge or entertainment. I ... with this statement because ...
>
> Think about ...

Self check

- Draft your paragraph first and then check it.
- Check that you have stated your opinion clearly. Do you agree or disagree? Have you given a reason or an example to support your opinion?
- Check that you have used some connectives to link your ideas.

CHALLENGE YOURSELF

Work in groups. To understand the importance of Gutenberg's invention, do some research on how information and knowledge was shared before we had the internet. Try to find other inventions, such as the fax machine, for example.

Each person in the group should try to find one invention and be able to say briefly what it was and how it worked.

Then report back to the group and try to rank each invention in terms of its importance or influence on our lives.

Speaking and listening

Opinions and arguments

Nikolas Tesla was a Serbian-American engineer who is sometimes credited with inventing the type of electrical **current** that we all use in our homes, alternating current or AC. Listen carefully to the opinions expressed about Tesla in Audio 7.4.

▲ Tesla invented the Tesla Coil. Do you know what that is? Find out

Try this

What is the writer's opinion about the work of Tesla? Choose the best answers.

1 Tesla is honoured in Croatia because ____________________.
- a he was a pioneering engineer
- b he set up a factory there
- c he invented a car which people still use today

2 Tesla set up his own company because ____________________.
- a he wanted to test X-rays on people
- b he wanted to try out his own ideas
- c he wanted to leave Croatia

3 Tesla was successful because ____________________.
- a he invented AC current which we use in our homes
- b he found a way to make the use of AC current easy and practical in electrical appliances
- c he invented X-rays

4 Tesla's ideas became well known because ____________________.
- a he made a lot of money and he used the money to advertise his ideas
- b he was the only person to work in this field
- c he was a showman who was good at explaining his ideas to the public

HINT

Remember that you must give reasons and examples to support your argument.

LET'S TALK

Work in groups. Listen to Audio 7.5 about the value of inventions and discuss the argument that is made in the text.

1 What does the writer say is the problem with inventions?
- a The inventions are not available to rich and poor alike.
- b The inventions are too complicated to be practical.
- c Inventions make the gap between the rich and the poor bigger.
- d Both a and c.

2 What do you think about the value of the World Wide Web? Prepare for a short debate on the subject in class. You can argue that the Web is valuable or that there is more to do to make the Web a valuable resource.

Writing

Research and write about a historical influencer

You are going to research and then write about a historical figure whom you believe has influenced the way we live today.

Work in groups.

1 Look at the photographs below and read how these people have become famous.

▲ Kalpana Chawla was the first woman from India to go up in a spaceship. Unfortunately, she died when the space shuttle Columbia exploded, but she inspired many women and girls to study science

▲ Wangari Maathai was an environmental activist who also won the Nobel Prize for Peace. She founded the Green Belt Movement, an environmental organisation focused on conservation, women's rights and planting trees in Kenya

▲ Begum Rokeya was a writer and educator who worked hard to promote education among women. She also wanted women and men to be treated equally. Her work is remembered every year in Bangladesh on 9 December – Rokeya Day

▲ Ada Lovelace was a mathematician in the nineteenth century. Many say she was the first computer programmer because she designed an algorithm to be used on a machine which was like a computer

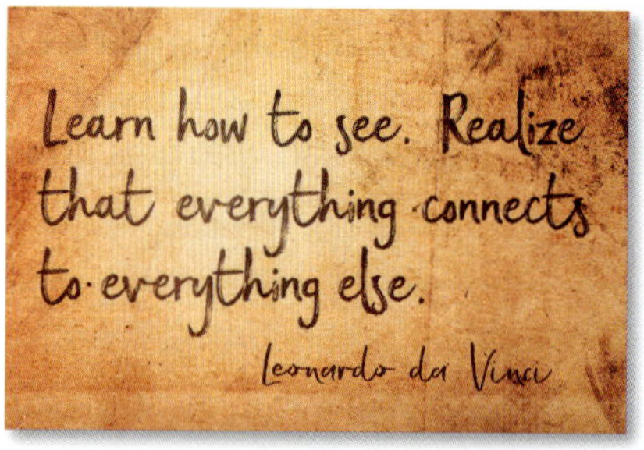

▲ Leonardo da Vinci worked in Europe in the fifteenth century. His interests and skills were wide ranging. He was a painter, sculptor, scientist, musician, engineer, botanist, cartographer (map maker) and inventor!

▲ Mohandas (Mahatma) Gandhi not only led India to independence, he also influenced people all over the world with his philosophy of peaceful resistance

2 Discuss the influence that you think these people may or may not have had. You may need to do some research at this point, but focus on the criteria that you think need to be applied to make someone an influencer. Here are some questions to think about:

- Why does this person need to be remembered?
- Is this person famous because they did something that interests us?
- Is this person famous because they were the first person to do something?
- Is the gender (male or female) of the person important?

PRACTISE

Choose one person and do further research about them. Then plan and write their biography. The biography should be about 200–250 words. It should be factual – check your facts – but you should also express an opinion about that person's influence.

Plan your biography, paragraph by paragraph. Draft your main or topic sentence for each paragraph first. Then add the detail.

HINT

Try to find a few quotes by the person you are researching. You can quote these words directly in quotation marks or write them in reported speech. Quotes give your reader a real idea of the person. To make your biography interesting, use direct and reported speech.

Self check

- Have you used quotes and are they written correctly?
- If you have used reported speech, have you checked the pronouns and verb tenses?
- Have you checked your facts?
- Have you checked your spelling?
- Have you stated an opinion about the person?
- Have you linked clauses to show the sequence of events and used the correct verb tenses (i.e. the past perfect and the simple past tense) to do this?

CHALLENGE YOURSELF

Write another paragraph about the same person in which you express a different point of view about that person's achievement.

For example, if you were writing about Nikolas Tesla's influence, you could express the view that other people used his ideas but he was the real genius behind the ideas, or you could argue that he was just a showman who was good at promoting ideas.

What can you do?

Read and review what you can do.

- I can listen to an interview and a podcast about people who have influenced us.
- I can talk about how we are influenced.
- I can read and listen to information about historical influencers and understand opinions.
- I can research and write about a historical influencer.
- I can use the past perfect tense in stories and in reported speech.

Now you have completed Unit 7, you may like to try the Unit 7 online knowledge test if you are using the Boost eBook.

8 Building a better future

In this unit you will:

- listen to a WhatsApp chat, a scientific discussion and a personal anecdote
- talk about **urbanisation**, and **environmental** and sustainable buildings
- read about sustainable buildings and how people adapt their buildings to their environment
- write a letter to a city official about improving the use of a local community area
- use the present perfect continuous tense, different noun phrases and prepositional phrases.

Speaking and listening

Where do you live?

1 Do you live in a city or in the countryside? Where would you most like to live, if you were able to choose? Discuss this in your groups. Use the pictures on the opposite page to help you.
   a What are the advantages of living in a city?
   b What are the disadvantages of living in a city?
   c What are the advantages of living in the countryside?
   d What are the disadvantages of living in the countryside?

2 Give the two photographs on the opposite page captions. Write them in your notebook.

3 Listen to Audio 8.1, as two cousins discuss a family visit that is planned. Citigirl lives in a big city. Greengro, her cousin, lives on a farm in a rural area. As you listen, see if you can find answers to these questions.
   a Where do you think Greengro lives? Think about the language he uses.
   b What kind of a girl is Citigirl? Think about how she feels about the compost toilet and needing her hairdryer.
   c Greengro teases his cousin a lot. What does he think of her? Does he like her?

PRACTISE

How would you say these sentences in a more formal way? Discuss this with a partner, and then write the sentences in your notebook. You can choose from some of the sentences in the box or write your own sentences.

1 How're you?
2 You've gotta be kidding!
3 Nope, for real.
4 C'mon, it'll be cool.

No, I am telling the truth.	You have got to be making a joke!
How are you?	Come on, it will be all right. We'll have fun.

CHALLENGE YOURSELF

What do you already know about?

- **Sustainable living**
- Compost toilets
- Solar panels

Choose one of the items listed and do some research on it. Write a simple description of the concept, and be prepared to explain it to the class in the next lesson.

Try this

1 Group these words into words for cities and words for countryside. What is the difference in meaning between each of the words?

metropolis	village	town	farm	suburb	municipality

2 Can you arrange the words in order, from the area with the most people in it, to the area with the least people in it?

Speaking and listening

Talking about towns

1 What does the word 'urbanisation' mean? Discuss it in your group.
   a Do you think urbanisation is good or bad? Or neither?
   b Look up the word 'urbanisation' in your dictionary. Write down the meaning in your notebook.

2 Listen to Audio 8.2, of Casey Brown interviewing an environmental scientist, Jane Hemingway, about urbanisation. Then discuss these questions.
   a Would you say Jane Hemingway is for or against urbanisation? Give reasons for your answer.
   b Is the talk show host for or against urbanisation?

3 Choose the correct answer to these questions, based on the interview you have just listened to. Work with a partner.
   1 Urbanisation means
      a making something more urban
      b people moving from one area to another
      c a population shift from rural areas to urban areas.
   2 What is the main reason people move to cities, according to Ms Hemingway?
      a The main reason is financial – they need to find jobs.
      b They want to live in a traffic-free zone.
      c They don't like farming.
   3 **Urban sprawl** is a term for
      a lying down in an urban area
      b setting up temporary homes on the **outskirts** of a city
      c not having much money.
   4 Jane studies urbanisation because
      a she wants to meet a fantastic urban planner
      b she wants to understand urban sprawl
      c she wants to learn how to understand cities better.

HINT

'To earn a living' is a way of saying you need to make enough money to live and support yourself and your family.

DID YOU KNOW?

There are 7.8 billion people living in the world!

Try this

Look at this photograph. Think of some of the problems a person may have, living in a very dense city centre like this.

- Discuss the problems with your partner.
- Make a list of problems people may have, living in a city.

Do you remember?

Debating

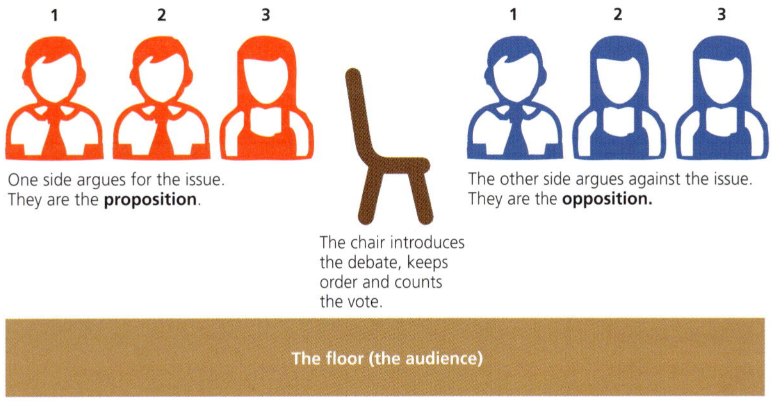

Try this

You are going to have a class debate. One half of the class will be arguing that living in a city is best; the other half will be arguing that living in a rural area is best. You will be put into a group, either 'City living' or 'Rural living'.

In your group, follow these steps.

1. First, prepare your argument. Divide your group into smaller groups to do research around an aspect of your topic, for example city living: culture, transport, shopping; rural living: fresh air, space, fresh produce.
2. Combine all your research into one document, and arrange your arguments in order of impact or importance.
3. Choose three people to represent your side of the argument.
   - The opening speaker will present your argument.
   - The second speaker will rebut the other team's opening speaker (argue against what the other group has said).
   - The third speaker will sum up your argument.
4. In between each stage, the speakers may seek advice from the group, before they return to the podium.
5. Have fun!

CHALLENGE YOURSELF

Write a paragraph giving your opinion of the matter under debate. Where do you think it's best to live (city or countryside), and why?

Use of English

Noun phrases

Sometimes just one noun is not enough to say what you want to say. For example:

They move to cities to find work.

Many people from other countries move to cities to find work.

Can you see that 'many people from other countries' is a noun phrase, that replaces the pronoun 'they'?

HINT

If you are unsure if a group of words is a noun phrase, see if it answers the question 'who?' or 'what?' in connection with the verb. It helps to underline the verb in the sentence, to start.

Do you remember?

The subject and object of a sentence are usually nouns. You can replace the noun with a noun phrase.

A noun phrase is a group of words (without a verb) that makes sense. For example:

Ordinary people like me need an expert to explain urbanisation.

People in the streets were queueing to get into the shop.

PRACTISE

1 Complete the sentences by using one of the noun phrases in these apartment blocks.

a My parents have moved to the countryside and they are getting used to ________________.

b Please put that into words that ________________ will understand.

c There are only ________________ available in rural areas.

d She is a ________________ by nature; she loves the hustle and bustle of a busy life.

e ________________ get rich, I'm afraid.

f ________________ are not all bad.

g ________________ study urbanisation in order to improve cities.

2 Use noun phrases to describe the photograph. For example:

The big, juicy strawberries grow in a plastic, semi-circular tunnel.

Present perfect continuous tense

The present perfect continuous tense is a verb tense that shows that an action has started in the past, and is still continuing in the present. It uses the form:

have been + -ing form of the verb

For example:

They have been living in the city for three years now.

I have been waiting for my lease for over two months.

She has been promising to send it for weeks, but she never does!

This tense emphasises that a certain amount of time has passed and that the action continues.

PRACTISE

Complete this letter by filling in the gaps with 'have been' or 'has been'. Write it in your notebook.

Dear Amina

I ________ waiting for your letter!

We ________ living in Abu Dhabi for three years now, and it feels like ages.

My father ________ working on one of the construction sites. You won't believe how much building there is going on in Abu Dhabi!

My sister ________ staying in the UK, while she finishes her degree.

I ________ wanting you to visit for ages!

We ________ putting together a list of things to do when you get here.

I'm looking forward to your visit.

Best wishes

Shamiela

Try this

Use the present perfect continuous form of the verb in brackets to complete these sentences.

1 I (study) architecture for the last three years.
2 He (travel) around the world looking at buildings for the last six months.
3 You (prepare) this talk for ages; don't be nervous!
4 They (wait) at the station for the high-speed train for 5 minutes.
5 You (plan) your new garden since last spring.
6 We (visit) the museum, while they (watch) a ball game.
7 She (find) it difficult to come up with a proper plan for her project.
8 He (help) her to set out the different parts of the project.

Reading

Read about an urban dream

1 If you were going to build your dream city, what would it look like? Discuss this in a group.
   a What essential services would you have? Think about water and electricity, for example.
   b Would you want a green, sustainable city? Why or why not?
   c How would people move from one place to another?
   d How would you adapt the design of your buildings to the environment in which you live?

2 Read about Masdar city, a futuristic city built in the desert near Abu Dhabi.
   a Do you know where Abu Dhabi is? Look it up on a map.
   b What is the climate like in Abu Dhabi?
   c How do you think a city would need to be adapted to suit this kind of climate?

Masdar city

Extract 1: The dream

In 2008, developers began building a new city near to Abu Dhabi in the United Arab Emirates. This city is known as Masdar city. Masdar city is created around the concept of environmental and sustainable living. All of the buildings were built using **recycled** materials, and the buildings were designed to use 40 per cent less water and energy than other buildings usually do. People would move around in driverless electric cars, similar to buses, rather than cars powered by fossil fuels.

The city is specially constructed to stay cool, as it is built at an angle to the sun to ensure that there is shade for most of the day. There is a special wind tower that redirects the cooler air from above the city into the city centre. All of these clever additions will help people to live more comfortably in a very hot climate.

The city is an example of how **innovation** and **collaboration** can help us to create more sustainable lifestyles and environments.

▲ The huge Teflon-coated wind tower channels cool breezes through the city

▲ Buildings have been designed with shade extensions

Extract 2: The world's first green ghost town?

▲ Electric cars move between the buildings

What happened to the dream? More than a **decade** has passed since they first began building at Masdar. It was such a good idea – a city built for **zero-carbon emissions**, made completely of recycled materials. This was a car-free city, with a plan for driverless **electric** cars that would act like buses – people could get in and out anywhere along the route. That plan came to an end after only two stops ended up being built. There is a giant Teflon-coated wind tower, cleverly constructed to channel cool breezes between the buildings.

Ten years on, only five per cent of the city has actually been built. There are well-designed buildings, including office blocks, a grocery store, a post office and coffee shops, but only 300 people live there. And they are the students at the Institute of Science and Technology, which is located in Masdar city.

A key problem may be that the city is 10 kilometres away from Abu Dhabi, and there is no transport system to get there. So you have to drive in your gas-guzzling car and then park in the parking lot before you can enter the city.

Is this the end of the dream? No, say the builders. The deadline for completing the city has been extended to 2030. It may not end up being 100 per cent zero-carbon, but it will be close they say. Let's hope this dream of a sustainable city comes true.

LET'S TALK

1 Work with a partner.
   a Read the two extracts again. Which of the promises made in extract 1 has not been fulfilled, if you then read extract 2?
   b Make a list of the inconsistencies between what was promised and what has actually been delivered.

2 Why do you think Masdar city has not been finished? Is it just the distance from the city of Abu Dhabi that is the problem, or do you think there might be other reasons? Discuss this in your group.

Dream vs reality

Answer these questions in your notebook.

Extract 1

1 Write down one sentence which explains what Masdar city is.
2 What is special about the buildings in Masdar city?
3 Why is the city built at an angle to the sun?
4 What is the function of the wind tower?
5 When did the construction of the city begin?

Extract 2

6 How much of the planned city has actually been built?
7 Which of the plans have not happened?
8 What do the 300 people who live in the city do?
9 Why is living in the city unsustainable?
10 Why do you think there is a difference in the way this city was promoted, and the reality of the city today?
11 Do you think the city will ever be finished? Why or why not?

Use of English

The language of building

If you want to ask a question in the present perfect continuous tense, you change the word order. For example:

I have been working on the plans for the last month.

Have you been working on the plans for the last month?

If you want to use the negative, you add 'not' to the verb. For example:

No, I have not been working on the plans for the last month.

▲ An architect planning a sustainable building

PRACTISE

1 Read this interview with an architect about what sustainable building is. As you read, find examples of the present perfect continuous tense. Write them down in your notebook.

Interviewer: For how long have you been working as an architect?

Architect: I've been working as an architect for almost ten years now.

Interviewer: That's impressive! We've been learning about sustainable buildings. Can you please explain what a sustainable building is?

Architect: Good question! I've been designing one for the city. Let me show you the plan.

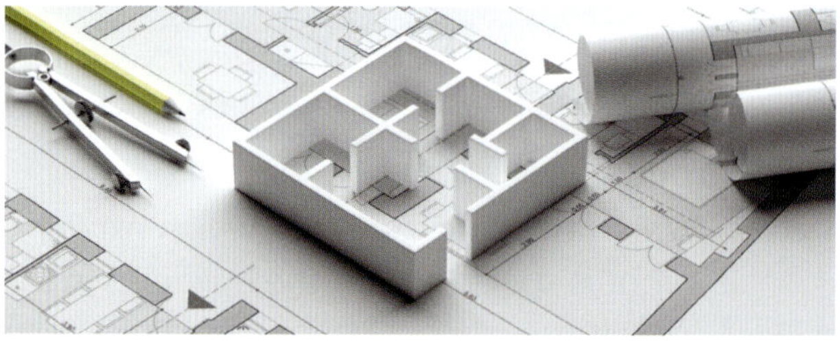

▲ The architect plans and builds a model of the **proposed** building

2 The interview continues. Can you find the noun phrases in this extract?

Architect: There are two ways to make a sustainable building. First, you can build with recycled materials. The use of recycled or **repurposed** materials is an element of sustainable building.

Interviewer: Is it an expensive way to build?

Architect: It can be, because most recycled materials have to be processed in some way, before they can be used. However, the real test of whether a building is sustainable or not, is the use of resources.

Interviewer: Can you explain that a bit more, please?

Architect: Sure. To make a building sustainable, you need to make sure it has its own energy and water supply. Rainwater is collected from the roof, then pipes carry this water down from the roof to water tanks, where it is stored to provide water for the building. A set of solar panels on the roof can provide electricity.

Building meaning with words

Do you remember?

Prepositional phrases consist of a preposition and a noun, or an adjective. For example: under construction, in time, by law, for a while.

In prepositional phrases, we use prepositions after nouns, adjectives and verbs, and we also use them before nouns and adjectives.

The preposition we use with each noun or adjective is important to the meaning. You need to learn to use certain prepositions with these nouns and adjectives. For example, a building is 'under construction' not 'in construction'.

PRACTISE

1 Work with a partner. Talk to each other about sustainable buildings. Try and use as many of these prepositional phrases as you can in your discussion.

on leave	by law	by the way	in fact		
	at speed	under construction	in debt	on schedule	
at a discount		on the air	according to		
	at the same time	by design	for sale	by accident	
on board		in a hurry	on paper		

2 Now choose five of the prepositional phrases. Write five sentences in your notebook, using these phrases.

▲ For a building to be really sustainable, it has to be part of a sustainable neighbourhood, district or town

Try this

1 Can you find the green spaces in the photograph? How would the town dwellers use these spaces?
2 What is in the big blue circle? What function do these objects serve?
3 Using the pictures and the interviews in this unit, write a short paragraph about how you would design a sustainable space – it could be a house, an office building or an open, green space. Try and use some of the grammar from this unit in your paragraph:
   - some prepositional phrases from the wall
   - some noun phrases, instead of one-word nouns.

Reading

Read about BIG buildings

1 Look at the photographs on the opposite page. All these buildings were built by an architect called Bjark Ingels and his company Bjark Ingels Group (BIG). Talk about the buildings.

- a What is the function of each building?
- b What is unusual about the buildings?
- c Would you like to visit these buildings? Say which one and explain why.

2 Before you read about some interesting buildings, learn the building language you will need to understand the text. The meanings of the words or phrases in this table are all mixed up. Match the word or phrase with its correct meaning.

Word or phrase	Meaning
boxy slab	pre-made, so the pieces can be put together easily on site
decent place to live	a very small amount of space on which to build
terraced	a watering system that collects all the rainwater, and then slowly drips it onto the plants
prefabricated	when one use of a building is mixed in with another use
limited space	have adjoining side walls
drip **irrigation**	a good place to live, that is attractive, has natural light, electricity and water
crossbreed	a big square slab of concrete

3 Read this case study about Danish architect Bjarke Ingels and his firm, BIG. As you read, think about these questions:

- a What are BIG's beliefs about buildings?
- b How do these beliefs influence the kind of buildings they make?

Bjarke Ingels and BIG

Bjark Ingels says, 'An apartment building doesn't have to look like a big boxy slab.' He believes that the building you live in creates a **framework** for your life, so it needs to add to the quality of your life. If you look at the apartment buildings in these photographs, you will see that each apartment has an outside area, with a garden or a balcony. His passion is to make housing that is both affordable and enjoyable to live in.

What is very impressive about all BIG's projects is how they use nature in their architecture, and they include features like gardens in all of their designs. This really helps to address two important challenges of city living: pollution and lack of access to nature.

▲ 79 & Park, a terraced, cedar-clad apartment block built around a park in Stockholm

This apartment block in Stockholm is called 79 & Park. It's a series of terraced apartments arranged on four sides around a **communal** park. The whole structure is made out of prefabricated modules. This means that it is designed to be made up of smaller sections that can be built and put together or removed without affecting the whole design. It's similar to building a structure out of children's building blocks. 79 & Park is designed to look like a hillside. Each little apartment has access to rooftop terraces or gardens, and the roof of the whole building is covered in small garden areas. There is plenty of outside space to enjoy.

▲ The Mountain, in Copenhagen

In Copenhagen, the BIG company created a building that they call 'The Mountain'. The challenge the company faced here was limited space. They needed to provide both parking and living space. Instead of creating two different blocks, they created one building that was **inspired** by the natural structure of a mountain. The architects put the parking below the apartments, like the base of the mountain, with the living spaces above the parking. All of the apartments have amazing views, and gardens that face the Sun. The building is cleverly designed to catch all the rainwater and use it in a drip-irrigation system that waters all the plants in the garden areas.

▲ CopenHill in Copenhagen

CopenHill is a sustainable power plant with a difference. BIG built a giant ski slope on the roof. There is also a public park area and a coffee shop, but the ski slope is the main attraction. It's the kind of building that really inspires. As Bjark Ingels says, why can't we crossbreed infrastructure, like power stations or bridges, so that it also has positive social and environmental effects?

4 Answer the questions.

a What does Bjark Ingels believe about building?

b What is impressive about each apartment block that BIG builds?

c How is the apartment block 79 & Park structured? If it is difficult to explain, you can draw a picture instead.

d What do 79 & Park and The Mountain have in common?

e What challenge did BIG face when they had to design The Mountain?

f How did they resolve this challenge?

g What is different about CopenHill?

h Do you think CopenHill is a well-designed building or not? Explain your answer.

DID YOU KNOW?

If you would like to find out more about BIG, and the interesting buildings they have created around the world, you can search for more information online. If you have an interest in design, and you would like to find out about other architects and designers, look out for the documentary series called *Abstract: The Art of Design*.

CHALLENGE YOURSELF

Design your own apartment block for families. Do a rough drawing of what your building will look like, give it a name, and add labels to indicate the apartments, and any gardens or other green space, balconies or shared parking spaces that there may be. What else will you include?

Speaking and listening

Listen to the story of an underground town

1 Look at the photographs on this page. Discuss them in your groups.
- a Where do you think this is? What in the photographs gave you a clue?
- b Why do you think people built houses underground?
- c Do you know of other places in the world where people live underground? Why did they choose to live underground? Share your knowledge with your group.
- d Would you like to live underground? Say why or why not.

2 Listen to Audio 8.3, the story of Coober Pedy. As you listen, answer these questions. Your teacher will play the audio twice.
- a Where is this town?
- b Would the speaker like to live there? Why or why not?
- c What does the speaker think about how the town looks, and why?
- d Why did the people build their homes like this? What is the speaker's opinion about this?
- e What is the town famous for?

▲ Coober Pedy is an old mining town. Here is what it looks like from above

▲ People used the old mining tunnels to make underground houses

LET'S TALK

Compare your summary notes with a partner's.

- Do you have the same notes about Coober Pedy? Add in information that you have left out, until your notes are complete.
- Write out a neat copy for your teacher.

Writing

▲ Write a letter to a community leader about improving a community area near you

▲ If you think that something could be improved, help make it happen! Give positive, active solutions that will help to solve the problem

Write a letter

Try this

You are going to write a letter to a local council or government official to highlight a problem in a community area and suggest a solution to that problem.

This could be a sports area that has been vandalised, a park that is not being properly cared for, an open plot that you think could be made into a communal area or a building that could be **renovated** to make it better-suited to the needs of your community.

Your letter needs to be a formal business letter. Use the writing frame below to help you.

Street
Town/City
Postcode/ZIP
← Write your address here.

00th Month 0000 ← Add the date here.

Write the name and title of the person you are writing to, and their address here. →
Recipient's name
Job title
Company name
Street
Town/City
Postcode/ZIP

Greet the person. → Dear ...

Put your topic here, and underline it. → Subject of letter

Introductory paragraph ← Write an introduction. It must say what you are concerned about, in brief, concise sentences. Keep your tone and language unemotional and stick to your point.

In this paragraph, say what effect this is having on the community. → Main paragraph ← Now give your well-thought-out solution. How you think this problem can be fixed or improved.

Thank the person for listening to you. → Conclusion to letter

Yours sincerely/faithfully

Sign and write your name. →
Signature
Your name

HINT

Use a more formal register for your letter, as you are writing to a government official.

Self check

- Have you followed the writing frame for your letter?
- Have you used a more formal register?
- Do you have three separate paragraphs outlining the problem, the effect on your community and your solution?
- Have you ended your letter correctly?

CHALLENGE YOURSELF

Is there a real need in your community that you can address as a class?

Work with your teacher to see if you can put this into action as a class, and provide some important community service.

What can you do?

Read and review what you can do.

- I can listen to a scientific discussion and a personal anecdote.
- I can talk about urbanisation, and environmental and sustainable buildings.
- I can read about sustainable buildings, and how people adapt their buildings to their environment.
- I can write a business letter to an official person expressing my ideas about improving the use of a local area for the community.
- I can use the present perfect continuous tense, different noun phrases and prepositional phrases.

Now you have completed Unit 8, you may like to try the Unit 8 online knowledge test if you are using the Boost eBook.

9 Our society

In this unit you will:

- listen to discussions about the rules at home, at school, on the playing field and in **society**
- talk about your ideal society and draw up, in groups, a plan for one particular aspect of your ideal society
- read about situations in which rules are changed because they are unfair or because of a crisis in society
- write a plan for your portfolio with your group and a self-evaluation paragraph about the experience of planning a new society
- use modal verbs and pronouns to discuss the laws of a just society.

RULES

- ✔ Always be kind
- ✔ Be respectful at all times
- ✔ Raise your hand to speak
- ✔ Ask questions
- ✔ Listen carefully
- ✔ Help each other
- ✔ Learn from mistakes
- ✔ Work quietly
- ✔ Play safely
- ✔ Always do your best

Speaking and listening

Whose rules are these?

1 Look at the sets of rules on the opposite page. Discuss them in your group.
   a Where do you think each of these sets of rules comes from?
   b How do you know this?
   c Are there rules that you would remove from these lists?
   d Are there rules that you would add to these lists?
   e Can you think of other places where there are rules?
   f Talk about what would happen if there were no rules in these places.
   g Share your ideas with the class.

2 Listen to Audio 9.1, a group of friends discussing rules they have at home.
   - As you listen, think about the rules you have in your home.
   - Make notes of the rules that you hear about and that you also have in your home.

3 Discuss your home rules with your group.
   - Which home rules do you think are **reasonable**? Why?
   - Which home rules would you change? Why?
   - Are there some home rules that you would like to have? What are they?

PRACTISE

Write down the rules you have in your home.

Use the forms: must/must not and have to. For example:

I must be home at 5:00 p.m.

I must not leave my dishes in the sink.

I have to help my parents with the laundry.

Speaking and listening

Listen and speak about rules

Listen to Audio 9.2, a general talk about rules and their importance. As you listen, find the correct answer to complete each of these sentences.

1 Society needs rules because
   a everyone would behave badly without them
   b someone has to be in charge
   c rules can keep us safe.
2 Informal rules
   a are rules that are written in informal language
   b are rules that help us to live together as a society
   c are rules for informal situations.
3 Formal rules
   a make up the laws of the land
   b are for formal occasions
   c are for school and classrooms.
4 If there were no rules at school
   a you could put up your hand and leave the classroom
   b it would be difficult for the teacher to teach and for learners to learn
   c you would not have to go to school.
5 If there were no rules on the football field
   a you would not be able to play the game
   b players could cheat
   c players would run away.

6 If there were no rules of the road
   a there would be some very bad accidents
   b it would be great – you could speed as much as you like
   c roads would remain safe places to be.
7 Do you have classroom rules? Work in a group.
   a Discuss your classroom rules.
   b What would you add to the rules?
   c What would you remove from the rules?
   d Keep notes on your ideas for the Use of English activity later.

HINT
Don't worry if you make a mistake during a discussion! We all do. Try to correct your mistake and continue speaking. If you are not sure of a word, ask your group for help.

The Island Nation challenge

CHALLENGE YOURSELF

You are the new rulers of a tropical island, inhabited by 20,000 people. In this activity, you are going to work as a class to decide how to govern the island.

▲ What will you call your Island Nation?

1 How well do you work together as a potential government? Let's find out by voting for a name for your new island.
   - Give suggestions for names to your teacher, who will write them on the board.
   - Vote on what to call your new island.

2 Have a class debate about what form of government you should have on the island. The rules are:
   - Your teacher's word is final, they may stop the debate at any time.
   - Think about what different roles you will need people to fill to make this new society work: who provides food, health, water, shelter, education, transport, etc.? How do they provide it? Who pays for it?

Government

- What kind of political system will you have?
- Will there be different political parties?
- Will people vote for the parties or for individual people?
- Will everyone have a vote?
- Is there a group who rule or does one person rule?
- How do the people who have to do the work of running the country get chosen?
- What departments are there in your government?

Once you have decided on a name for your country and a system of government, you can continue to the next step.

3 Your teacher will divide you into different groups. Each group is in charge of one portfolio for your government.
   - Get into your group and read over the card your teacher has given you.
   - For homework, you might like to find out more about your portfolio. Who runs this portfolio in your country? What rules, or laws, have they made?

HINT

Portfolio – a range of responsibilities held by a particular group of people.
So, if your portfolio is 'Transport', you will have to draw up rules and plans for transport.

Use of English

Using the language of the law

Now, you're going to learn to write rules and laws for your new island country. There are some useful ways of using English that will help you.

- You can use modal verbs, for example:

You must not steal.

- You can use indefinite pronouns. For example:

Everyone has to pay their taxes on time. (You don't need to mention people by name.)

- You can use the passive voice. For example:

Rules will be enforced at all times. (Use if you don't want to, or have to, say by whom.)

Do you remember?

Modal verbs are helping verbs that are added to the main verb. They are very useful when talking about laws and rules.

- Must and have to are about **obligation**, for example: 'You must be home by 6.'
- Should gives advice and opinion, for example: 'She should not tease him so much.'
- May and might show possibility, for example: 'Someone might get hurt.'
- Can and could show ability, for example: 'He can go to soccer as soon as this is over.'
- Would is a more polite word for obligation, for example: 'Would you help your grandmother, please?'

Try this

Remember your classroom rules from earlier?

1. Look at your notes. Compare them with your group's notes.
2. Make one complete set of classroom rules in your group.
3. Make sure you use a modal verb for each rule.
4. Write your rules out neatly on a poster. Decorate your poster.
5. Display your posters in the classroom.

PRACTISE

Add a modal verb from the 'Do you remember?' box to complete each of these sentences. There may be more than one possible answer. Write them in your notebook.

1. If you break the law, you ______ go to jail.
2. Laws ______ make things fair in society.
3. If you want to ask the teacher a question, you ______ put up your hand.
4. It ______ be difficult to play soccer without rules.
5. Players ______ get hurt if there are no rules.
6. Accidents ______ happen if people drove all over the road.
7. It ______ be good to start a new country, with new laws.
8. I ______ make myself president, but we will see!

Keeping it general

Do you remember?

Pronouns

Indefinite pronouns refer to people in a general way. They are indefinite in number, for example: some, one, anyone, someone, everyone, no one.

Everyone can vote in my country.

No one is allowed to break the law.

Quantitative pronouns indicate an indefinite **quantity** (or item) – some, any, none, one, much, many, little, few.

You have so many ideas, may I borrow one?

In our country there are many rules; we obey most.

Now use a pronoun from the 'Do you remember?' box, or your own choice of pronoun, to complete these sentences.

1 ________ has to wash their hands before they eat lunch.
2 Do you want this food? I have ________ left over.
3 She loves parties, but she is not allowed to go to ________.
4 ________ has different rules at home.
5 I like the class rules; I would not change ________.
6 ________ understands what it is like to live in my house!
7 Some rules are formal; ________ are not.
8 ________ can be elected president, if he or she gets enough votes.

CHALLENGE YOURSELF

Work in your Island Nation groups and discuss the questions under 'Think about' on the card your teacher gave you.

- Use the indefinite pronouns in the 'Do you remember?' box in your discussion, for example:

Everyone should be responsible.

Will there be houses for all?

- Use modal verbs when you are drawing up your plans, for example:

People must not steal.

Everyone should pay for electricity and water.

- Make notes as these will form the basis of the policy and goals for your group.

Reading

Read about breaking unfair rules

Not all rules are right, or good, or benefit most of society. Throughout history, there have been brave people who have stood up to unfair laws.

Votes for women

In nineteenth-century New Zealand, as in a lot of societies, women were excluded from any involvement in politics and they were not allowed to vote. Many people felt this was unfair, and they campaigned for women's rights to have their say. The movement to allow women to vote is called the women's suffrage movement. In New Zealand, this movement was led by a woman named Kate Sheppard. She travelled around the country holding public meetings and making speeches, campaigning for the rights of women and writing to newspapers. She started a petition to show the members of Parliament just how many people wanted the laws to change – when she unrolled this completed petition in front of the New Zealand Parliament it was 270 metres long and had nearly 32,000 signatures on it! All her work paid off; in 1893, New Zealand passed the Electoral Act and became the first country in the world to give women the vote. This was known as 'universal suffrage' because now everyone could vote, as long as they were old enough. It inspired other suffrage movements all over the world.

▲ Kate Sheppard, a leader in the New Zealand Women's Suffrage Movement, featured on a NZ$10 note

1 Discuss these questions in your groups.
   a Why do you think it took such a long time for women to be given the vote?
   b How would you choose to show your feelings about a law you do not think is right? Use the structure, I would/I would not/I wouldn't, in your answer.

2 Nelson Mandela was one of the men who stood against apartheid in South Africa. He was fighting for equal laws for black people and white people.
   a Read part of the speech that he made, before he was thrown into prison for 27 years.
   b Which laws was Nelson Mandela most worried about?

HINT
Nelson Mandela used the word 'African' in his speech, which was the correct terminology for the 1960s to refer to only black South Africans. Today we use the term 'African' for anyone born in Africa, and we identify different groups as black and white.

South Africa is the richest country in Africa, and could be one of the richest countries in the world. But it is a land of extremes and remarkable **contrasts**. The white people of South Africa enjoy what may well be the highest standard of living in the world, whilst black people live in **poverty** and **misery** …

… There are two ways to break out of poverty. The first is by formal education, and the second is by the worker acquiring a greater skill at his work and thus higher wages. As far as black South Africans are concerned, both these avenues of advancement are deliberately **curtailed** by **legislation**.

I ask the Court to remember that the present Government has always sought to **hamper** black people in their search for education. One of their early acts, after coming into power, was to stop **subsidies** for black South Africans' school feeding. Many black South African children who attended schools depended on this supplement to their diet. This was a cruel act.

There is **compulsory** education for all white South African children at virtually no cost to their parents, be they rich or poor. Similar facilities are not provided for the black South African children.

▲ Nelson Mandela, and many other people, fought for the rights of black people in South Africa. It took over 30 years, but eventually the people won

Vocabulary

1 Look up these words in your dictionary. Write the words and their meanings in your notebook.

- poverty
- subsidy
- legislation
- misery
- advancement

Say the words out loud. Make sure the stress falls on the correct syllable. Learn to spell the words.

2 Read the passage again and answer the questions.

a Write down two ways that a person could overcome poverty, according to this speech. (paragraph 2)

b Why could African people not follow these two ways, according to Mandela? (paragraph 2)

c What was one of the first things the Apartheid government did when it came into power? (paragraph 3)

d Which children got compulsory education in 1964? (paragraph 4)

▲ Black children did not have access to good education in the Apartheid era. The children themselves rebelled against these bad rules in the Soweto uprising of 1976

LET'S TALK

Can you think of some instances of unfair rules or laws, either today or in the past? What makes a rule unfair? Talk about this with your partner.

Use of English

Using language to protect society

Sometimes a huge danger to society may mean we have to change the way we live.

The coronavirus (Covid-19) pandemic of 2019/20 shocked the world. Within months, the virus had spread all around the globe. Every country had to decide how to deal with the Covid-19 virus. Every country had to change their laws to keep their people safe.

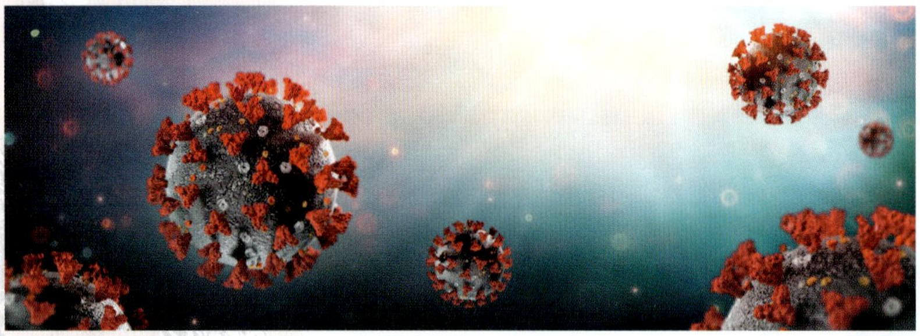

▲ Covid-19 is a highly infectious virus

PRACTISE

Read the information below which the United Kingdom published at the time that Covid-19 was spreading rapidly. (source: www.nhs.uk)

1 Work with a partner. Find all the modal verbs in the text and write them down.

2 Now find the indefinite pronouns and write them down.

- Stay at home!
- You must only leave your house for food, to go to a pharmacy or doctor, or for work if you are not able to work from home.
- If you go out, you must always stay 2 metres (6 ft) away from others.
- You must wash your hands as soon as you get home.
- You should not meet any friends or family.
- Remember that even if you don't have symptoms, you could have the virus. You must **minimise** your contact with everyone.
- Non-essential businesses must close. Any places serving food, like restaurants, cafés and pubs, must only sell takeaway food.
- You must only leave the house to exercise once per day.
- If you are a critical worker, such as a doctor or nurse, you can leave the house to go to work. Other critical workers include police people, social workers and people who work in banks.
- You should not gather in a public place with more than one other person.
- You can go to help elderly or vulnerable loved ones by dropping groceries or medication at their door.
- You must not move house during the virus, as far as possible.

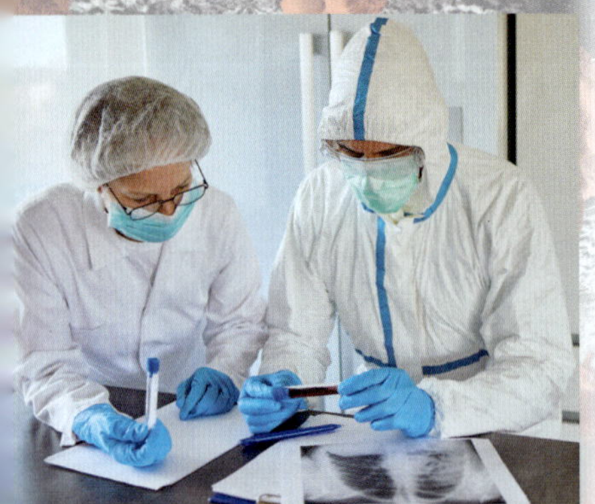

▲ Scientists have worked round the clock to help find a vaccine for the virus

Staying safe

Try this

1 Read this infographic about Covid-19.
   a Talk about what new rules your country made and advice that was given during the time of Covid-19.
   b Were the rules the same as the ones on the infographic?
   c What other rules did you have?

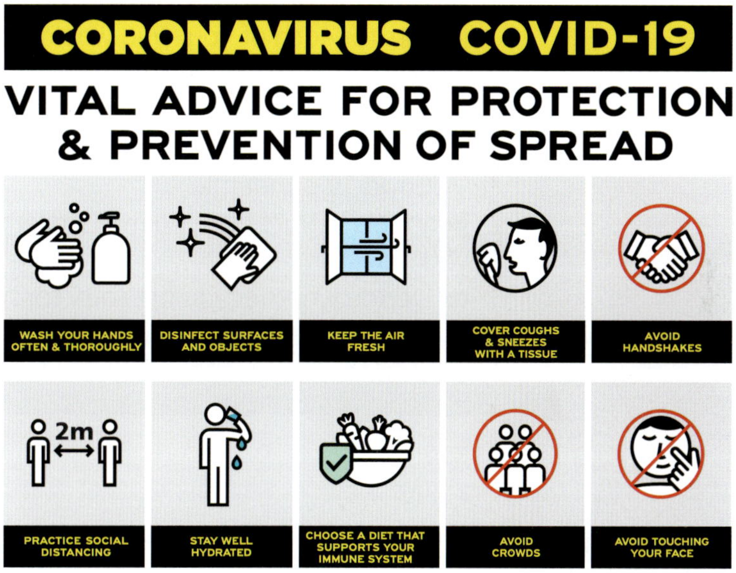

2 Rewrite the advice in the infographic into more formal rules. Use modal verbs and indefinite pronouns to do this. For example:

Everyone must wash their hands often, and thoroughly.

Do you remember?

Indefinite pronouns: everybody, everyone, no one, all, some, someone, others

Modal verbs: must, have to, can, could, should, might, may

Try this

Write a short paragraph about how Covid-19 affected you and your community. What is the main thing you remember about lockdown?

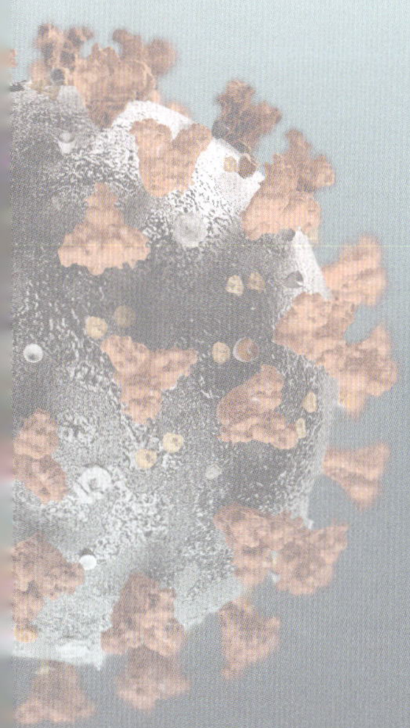

CHALLENGE YOURSELF

1 Your group wrote rough notes about your portfolio for your Island Nation in the last 'Use of English' lesson. Now, it is time to refine those notes.
   a First check that the language and spelling is correct.
   b Make sure you have used modal verbs in your laws or list of instructions.
   c Select the person with the best handwriting to write your plans out neatly.

2 Now, look at the 'Consult' instructions on your card. Later you will have to consult the various teams mentioned on the card. (This excludes the **treasury** group.)
   a Plan your approach. What do you need from the other teams, in order to do your job properly?
   b Make a list of your requirements, so you are ready for the meetings.
   c Leave some space on your clean copy of the plans, in case you need to add anything new, after your consultation.

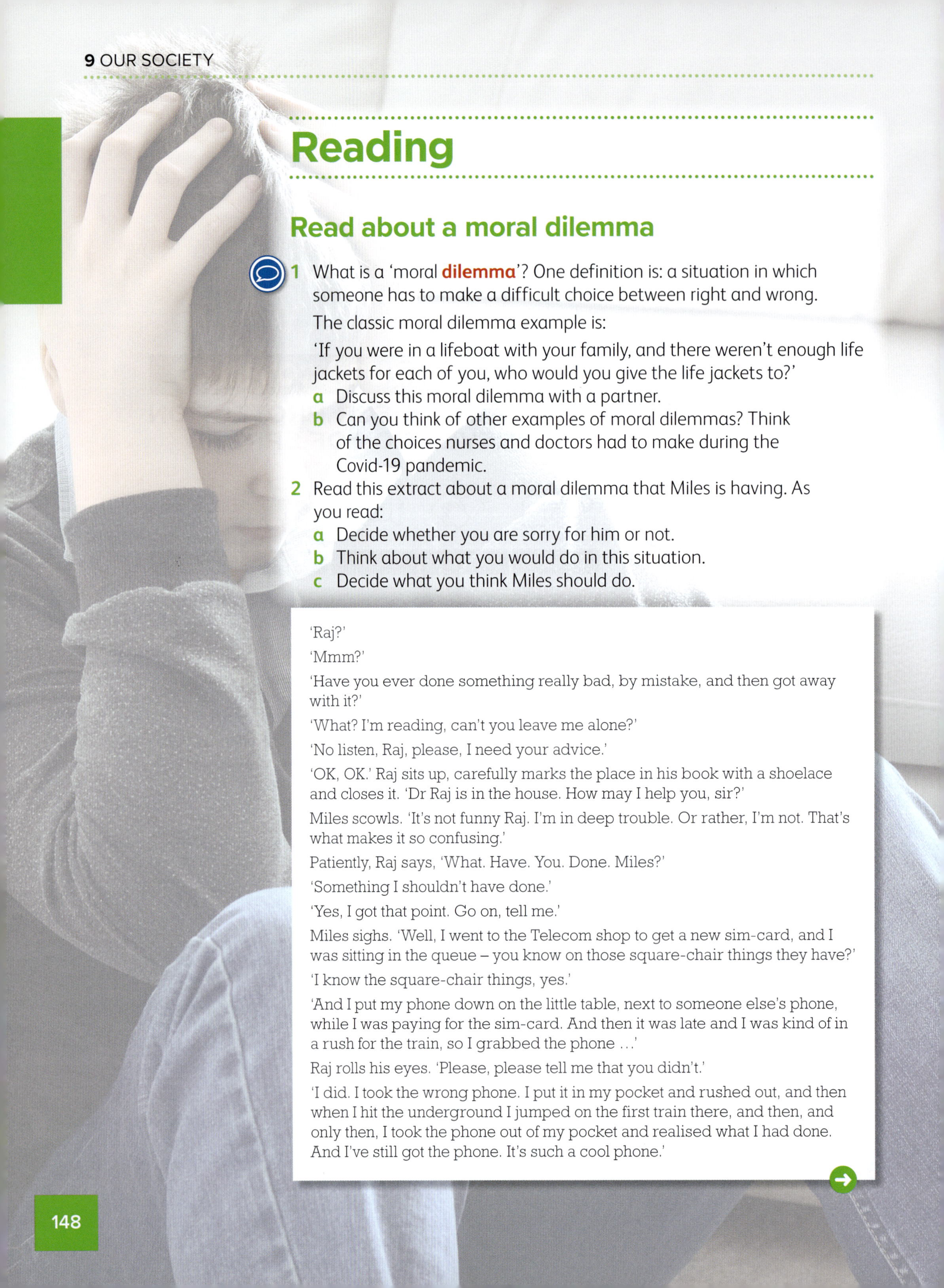

Reading

Read about a moral dilemma

1 What is a 'moral **dilemma**'? One definition is: a situation in which someone has to make a difficult choice between right and wrong.

The classic moral dilemma example is:

'If you were in a lifeboat with your family, and there weren't enough life jackets for each of you, who would you give the life jackets to?'

a Discuss this moral dilemma with a partner.

b Can you think of other examples of moral dilemmas? Think of the choices nurses and doctors had to make during the Covid-19 pandemic.

2 Read this extract about a moral dilemma that Miles is having. As you read:

a Decide whether you are sorry for him or not.

b Think about what you would do in this situation.

c Decide what you think Miles should do.

'Raj?'

'Mmm?'

'Have you ever done something really bad, by mistake, and then got away with it?'

'What? I'm reading, can't you leave me alone?'

'No listen, Raj, please, I need your advice.'

'OK, OK.' Raj sits up, carefully marks the place in his book with a shoelace and closes it. 'Dr Raj is in the house. How may I help you, sir?'

Miles scowls. 'It's not funny Raj. I'm in deep trouble. Or rather, I'm not. That's what makes it so confusing.'

Patiently, Raj says, 'What. Have. You. Done. Miles?'

'Something I shouldn't have done.'

'Yes, I got that point. Go on, tell me.'

Miles sighs. 'Well, I went to the Telecom shop to get a new sim-card, and I was sitting in the queue – you know on those square-chair things they have?'

'I know the square-chair things, yes.'

'And I put my phone down on the little table, next to someone else's phone, while I was paying for the sim-card. And then it was late and I was kind of in a rush for the train, so I grabbed the phone …'

Raj rolls his eyes. 'Please, please tell me that you didn't.'

'I did. I took the wrong phone. I put it in my pocket and rushed out, and then when I hit the underground I jumped on the first train there, and then, and only then, I took the phone out of my pocket and realised what I had done. And I've still got the phone. It's such a cool phone.'

Raj looks truly shocked. 'I can't believe it Miles, I mean, you're a straight-A student, you want to be a biochemist when you finish school, and save the world from evil viruses, and now you've just messed up BIG TIME.'

Miles puts his head in his hands. 'I know, I know. Don't shout!'

'So what are you going to do?'

Miles looks up. 'See, that's the tricky thing, Raj. I know I should take it back. But no one knows that I took it. Except you, I mean.'

Raj stands up. Miles scoots back on his bed. 'You must take it back, Miles; you have to. You know that. You can explain and it will all end up being all right.'

Miles clamps his hands over his head. 'Must, must, should, have to, could, won't! Aaarrrgghh!' He screams.

'Is everything all right in there?' his mother asks, popping her head round the door.

'Fine,' they both say quickly.

Try this

Answer these questions in your notebook.

1 What is Miles' moral dilemma?

2 How do you think Raj feels about this? Write down one sentence from the text which explains his feelings.

3 In what order did events happen? Use words from the box to complete the explanation of the sequence of events.

__________, Miles went to the shop. __________, he put his phone on the table next to someone else's phone while he paid for the sim-card. __________, he picked up the wrong phone and put it in his pocket. __________, he rushed out of the shop to catch his train. __________ he told his friend Raj.

then quickly finally first next

4 Why is Raj truly shocked?
- a Because Miles is confused.
- b Because Miles went to the Telecom shop.
- c Because Miles is usually a good person.

5 What does Raj want Miles to do?
- a Tell no one what happened.
- b Explain that he picked up the wrong phone by mistake.
- c Jump on the first train out of there.

6 Why does Miles shout 'Must, must, should, have to, could, won't! Aaarrrgghh!'?
- a Because he is practising his grammar.
- b Because he doesn't know what to do.
- c Because he knows what to do, but doesn't want to do it.

7 What do you think happens next?
- Write the last paragraph of this story.
- You can choose any ending you like.

Speaking and listening

Listen and speak about your Island Nation

In this activity, you are going to:

- consult with the various groups that you need to
- regroup to add any new items to your written plans
- present the plans for your group's Island Nation to the class.

LET'S TALK

Your class has been divided into the following groups, each responsible for one of your Island Nation's government portfolios.

- On the teacher's instruction, move to another table to consult with members of the other groups who are responsible for the same portfolio as you. Add new information to your plans, based on your consultations.
- Regroup and finalise your plans.
- Present your plans to the class. Everyone in the group should be part of the spoken presentation.

HINT

Remember! If you make a mistake, try to correct the mistake and then continue speaking.

Treasury

You decide how the money the government has gathered through taxes is going to be spent. This is a serious responsibility.

- **Action:** You have $500,000,000 to run the country for a year. You need to budget for: education, city services, the legal system, officers of the law, business and industry, and cultural affairs.
- Decide how to split your budget between these departments. Write down the decisions you have made and give reasons for each decision.
- **Think about:** What does the treasury pay for, and what do individuals, business and industry pay for?
- The other teams are going to come to you for funding, so draw up your budget and be prepared to negotiate!

Legal system

You are the people who draw up the laws for the country.

- **Action:** Decide on the **fundamental** laws for the country. Write them down. You should have at least ten laws.
- **Think about:** What does the government control, and what do people get to decide on their own? Are there jails? Are there courts?
- **Consult:** The officers of the law to see how they will enforce your laws.
- **Consult:** The treasury, for any money you may need.

Officers of the law

You are the people who decide how the laws of the country are carried out.

- **Action:** Draw up a plan for a law enforcement agency. Your plan should have at least ten points in it.
- **Think about:** Do the people carrying out the law have guns? Who decides on right and wrong? What happens if someone breaks a law? Are there jails? Are there courts?
- **Consult:** The legal system, as together you need to decide how the law is to be carried out.
- **Consult:** The treasury, for any money you may need.

City services

You provide water, electricity and waste removal.

- **Action:** Decide how you are going to supply these services. Write up a description of your services. You should have at least three points for each service.
- **Think about:** Who pays for these services? How do they pay (e.g. monthly, or buy on a voucher system)? How do people access the services? Does everyone have access to the services? Is there a difference if the services apply to a person or a business?
- **Consult:** The legal system, for any laws you need put into place around services.
- **Consult:** The treasury, for any money you may need.

Business and industry

You are responsible for economic matters – business and industry.

- **Action:** Decide which business and industries there will be. Write up a description of what they are. There should be at least ten main points in your description.
- **Think about:** Will business and industry be private, and organised and paid for by the business owners? Will any industries be run by the government (e.g. transport, communications)? How will people be paid in this case?
- **Consult:** The legal system, for any laws you need put into place around industry and business.
- **Consult:** The treasury, for any money you may need.

Cultural affairs

You are responsible for the press, cultural affairs and sports.

- **Action:** Write up your plans. You should have at least three points for each aspect of your responsibilities.
- **Think about:** Is there any censorship? Is the press allowed to report on everything? Which religions do you have? What is the national sport?
- **Consult:** The legal system, for any laws you need put into place around censorship or religion.
- **Consult:** The treasury, for any money you may need for cultural venues, like theatres, or sports stadia.

Education

You get to decide what kind of education system the country will have.

- **Action:** Write down what happens at primary school, high school and post-school. You should have at least three points for each aspect of education.
- **Think about:** What kind of education system do you have? Do you have free basic education, paid for by government? Is education private? How do people train to become plumbers, electricians, etc.? Are there universities? How is post-school education paid for – by parents or by government?
- **Consult:** The legal system, for any laws you need put into place around compulsory education, etc.
- **Consult:** The treasury, for any money you may need for schools, technical colleges, school fees, etc.

Writing

Write a plan for your Island Nation

Each group has their instructions for writing the plan for their portfolio:

- Treasury
- Legal system
- Officers of the law
- City services
- Cultural affairs
- Business and industry
- Education

Try this

Use this checklist to proofread your group text, before you hand in a neat copy to your teacher.

Checklist

Grammar and vocabulary

- [ ] Properly constructed sentences
- [ ] A variety of appropriate vocabulary

Punctuation

- [ ] Full stops at the end of sentences
- [ ] Sentences starting with capital letters

Spelling

- [ ] All words checked and spelled correct
- [ ] Used a dictionary to check spellings and meanings of words

Format/layout

- [ ] Each separate point of the plan is clearly marked
- [ ] Each point is numbered
- [ ] Spaces between paragraphs

Content

- [ ] Information properly researched and consulted on with the appropriate groups
- [ ] Information is organised logically

HINT

- Make sure you have used modal verbs in your rules and laws.
- Make sure you've used indefinite pronouns, like all, some, everyone, etc.
- Well done on such a complicated group task!

Self check

Write a short paragraph about your experience of the Island Nation project.

- What did you like about it?
- What did you not like about it?
- Were you able to get your ideas heard by your group?
- How do you think the project turned out, as a whole?
- How could the project be improved for the next class that tries it?
- What did you learn from doing this project?

What can you do?

- I can listen to discussions about the rules at home, at school, on the playing field and in society.
- I can talk about an ideal society and draw up, in my group, a plan for one particular aspect of our ideal society.
- I can read about situations in which rules are changed because they are unfair, or because of a crisis in society.
- I can write a plan for our group portfolio, and a self-evaluation paragraph about the experience of planning a new society.
- I can use modal verbs and pronouns to discuss the laws of a just society.

Now you have completed Unit 9, you may like to try the Unit 9 online knowledge test if you are using the Boost eBook.

Review Units 7–9

PRACTISE

Choose words from the box to connect these sentences. Sometimes you may have to change the order of the sentences, so that the events are in the right order.

so that	although	so	before	that
but	if	while	however	even if

1 He had been a champion video gamer. He went to university.
2 I follow about a hundred influencers on social media. My sister doesn't.
3 She wants to live in one of his buildings. She admires Bjark Ingels so much.
4 It seems so impractical. I love the idea of a ski slope on top of a power station.
5 Every society needs rules. It can function properly.
6 They wanted to learn about coding. They asked the supply teacher to teach them HTML.
7 I really admire Tank Man. I would never be able to do what he did.
8 There are no rules at school. It would be difficult for teachers to teach.
9 She waits to hear from the university. She is studying computer science.
10 My mother looked after all of us and made us a lovely, safe home. I never want to be a housewife.

Try this

Work in pairs. Change this dialogue to reported speech.

Jason: Have you done the assignment for History today?

Melissa: I finished it yesterday, but it's not very good.

Jason: Why do you say that?

Melissa: Because I'm not very interested in Greek philosophers. If the assignment had been about coding, I would be top of the class!

Jason: I need good marks on this one. I am a bit behind this year.

Melissa: Jason, you will be fine! Don't worry so much. Do you have time for a coffee now?

Jason: Can we make it next time? I need to finish this before Maths class.

LET'S TALK

You learned about the town Coober Pedy in Unit 7. In your group, discuss the kinds of rules you would need to have in an underground town. Write down ten rules that you decide on collectively. Use modal verbs in each rule (must, have to, should, would, etc.).

▲ The entrances to several homes in Coober Pedy

PRACTISE

Use the present perfect continuous form of the verb in brackets to complete the sentences.

1 He (study) in the library for two hours.
2 She (work) on her philosophy project since last week.
3 Can you believe we (live) in Dubai for three years already?
4 They (mine) opals at Coober Pedy since the start of the twentieth century.
5 I (concentrate) on my Island Nation project, so I forgot to finish my Maths homework.
6 People (dig) up old ruins in Egypt for many years.
7 Where (live) you for the last five years?
8 No, they not (help) us with this project.
9 Can we go now? You (eat) the same spoonful of pudding for hours!
10 I (wonder) what to study when I leave school.

PRACTISE

In Unit 9, you worked as a class to plan your ideal Island Nation. Choose one aspect of the government that you discussed as a class and write your own views about this. You can use the findings of the group you were in or choose another aspect that interests you. Choose from:

- Legal system
- Treasury
- Officers of the law
- City services
- Education
- Business and industry
- Cultural affairs.

Draft a short explanation of your views in two paragraphs.

Paragraph 1: Say how you think this aspect of the nation should be managed.

Paragraph 2: Give your reasons for your position.

CHALLENGE YOURSELF

Write a leaflet describing this building to potential buyers. Mention all the features of the building that buyers would be interested in. Use as many descriptive noun phrases as you can, for example: custom-designed housing, city dwellers, etc.

◀ The Mountain, in Copenhagen

Glossary

accommodation (noun) a room, group of rooms or building in which someone may live or stay

advantage (noun) a better position, or the good results gained from something

advertising (noun) the job or business of creating and distributing advertisements, which are public notices that tell people about products, services or events

algorithm (noun) a process or set of rules to be followed in calculations or other problem-solving operations, especially by a computer

anecdote (noun) a short story about a funny or interesting event

anxious (adjective) feeling worried, nervous or afraid about something uncertain, or the future

apartment (noun) a room or set of rooms used as living space

associate (verb) to connect something with something else in your mind

at least (phrase) at the lowest amount; not less than. Or, in any case; at any rate

authentic (adjective) real, genuine or true

awe (noun) a very strong feeling of wonder mixed with respect or fear

barrier (noun) anything that gets in the way of progress or success

belong (verb) to be accepted as part of a group, to fit in somewhere, to be a part of something

benefit (noun) anything that does someone good or gives someone an advantage

benefit (verb) to be helpful to or give good results to something

bilingual (adjective) someone who speaks two languages very well or fluently

bleach (verb) to make white or lighter in colour by using a chemical or sunlight

border (noun) the edge or boundary for something, or the line that divides two countries

boycott (noun) a protest where you refuse to buy products, use products or services, or go to events, in an effort to bring about change

boycott (verb) refusing to buy products, use products or services or go to events, in protest

budget (noun) a plan for how much money will be spent and earned during a certain period

bungee jump (noun phrase) a recreational activity in which a person harnessed to the end of a long, anchored, elasticised rope, or bungee, steps off a height, rapidly drops hundreds of feet in the air, then bounces up and back down, repeatedly, while the movement gradually slows to a stop

campaign (noun) a series of planned actions carried out in order to reach a particular goal, for example an advertising campaign

campsite (noun) a place where one sets up a tent or camper for camping, usually within a campground

causeway (noun) a raised road or path across water or wet land

cave (noun) a natural hole or hollow in the earth; many caves have openings in a hillside or cliff

ceremony (noun) a formal act or series of actions done in a particular way to honour a special occasion, for example a wedding ceremony

character(s) (noun) a person in a story, play or movie

civil rights (noun phrase) the rights given by a nation's government to all its citizens. In the USA, certain rights, such as the right to vote, own property and have a fair trial are guaranteed by the Constitution and Acts of Congress. Martin Luther King was a leader in the fight for civil rights for African Americans

co-operative (noun) a project that is owned and run by several people, such as a farming co-operative

coding (noun) the process of assigning a code to something for the purposes of classification or identification. In computer programming, coding refers to creating programming code for computers

collaboration (noun) a co-operative effort by which people or organisations work together to accomplish a common project or mission

column (noun) an upright structure that looks like a post. A column helps support a building

communal (adjective) something that relates or belongs to members of a community, public or collective

compulsory (adjective) something that is required or necessary

concrete (noun) a hard, strong building material made by mixing sand, gravel, cement and water

connect (verb) to join together or associate one thing with another

connection (noun) something that connects, or the act of connecting. Something that is related or joined to something else

contrasts (verb) to show or reveal differences when compared

crossbreed (noun) a hybrid organism produced by crossbreeding, or breeding two different varieties of the same species

crow (noun) a shiny black bird known for its shrill, harsh cry. Crows are often seen looking for food

crowded (adjective) very full, or too full, of things or people

current (noun) the flow of electricity in a wire or other conductor

curtailed (verb) to make something shorter or cut off part of it

decade (noun) a unit of time equal to ten years

declutter (verb) to remove mess or clutter from (a place)

descend (verb) to move downward or to a lower position. Or, to be related by blood through several generations

developed (verb) to bring out the potential of something, or to advance to a more complete or more effective condition

dilemma (noun) a situation that requires a choice between two actions, neither of which will be a good solution

disturb (verb) to interrupt, especially by making noise. Or, to trouble someone or something, or to make someone nervous or uneasy

donate (verb) to give in order to help a charity or other group

dye (noun) a substance that is used to give colour to cloth, hair or other materials

dye (verb) to colour or stain by soaking in dye

effect (noun) a result or change that is produced by an action or another cause

electric (adjective) something that works by using or gives off electricity

emissions (noun) the production and discharge of something, especially gas or radiation, for example carbon emissions

environmental (adjective) of or having to do with the surroundings of something, especially the natural surroundings

exist (verb) to be alive, to live or to be real

exploitation (noun) the selfish or unfair use of someone or something for one's own advantage

fantasy (noun) imagination or something that is imagined. A fantasy story is very imaginative and contains strange characters, places or events

field (noun) an area of special activity or interest

fit (verb) to be the right shape and size for. For example, the battery fits in the remote

flock (verb) to gather together or travel in a crowd or large group

fluent (adjective) to be able to speak, write or understand well

forge (verb) to move forward gradually but with strength of purpose

forge (verb) to invent or imitate in order to deceive. For example, forging someone's signature

framework (noun) a structure that supports something built on or around it

fundamental (adjective) something that is basic, central or serves as a foundation

gap (noun) a space or opening made by or as if breaking or separating

generation (noun) an entire group of people who were born around the same time. For example, your grandparents' generation

genre (noun) a particular type, sort or category. In art, this is often marked by a particular specified form, technique or content

GIF (noun) a type of computer file that contains a still or moving image. GIF is the abbreviation for 'Graphic Interchange Format'

glacier (noun) a large mass of ice formed in cold regions from compacted snow, which moves very slowly down a slope or across land

griot (noun) a West African storyteller, historian and entertainer who traditionally preserves, remembers and performs the historical stories of their people

guard (noun) a person who watches out for danger or protects property

guard (verb) to watch over something to protect it, or to prevent harm or escape

hamper (verb) to get in the way of something

hashtag (noun) a word or phrase preceded by the hash sign (#), used in social media to identify or search for a particular topic

heights (noun) a high place from which one can look out

hereditary (adjective) something that has to do with characteristics that are passed or could be passed from parent to offspring

home language (noun phrase) the language that someone grew up listening to and speaking at home

household (noun) the group of people, such as a family, that lives in a house

illegal (adjective) something that is against the law or rules

imply (verb) to hint or suggest without saying directly

influential (adjective) having power or influence

injustice (noun) an act that is not just, not legal or not moral. Something that is wrong

innovation (noun) a new idea, product or way to do something

inspire (verb) to cause someone to do something or to stimulate or influence (someone to do something) by stirring the emotions

irrigation (noun) the supplying of water to land by man-made means

laser (noun) a device that makes a strong, narrow beam of light by stimulating the atoms in a gas or crystal

legislation (noun) a law made by a body of government

literally (adverb) something that is real, or a fact

logistics (noun) the planning and implementing of the details of any operation

mechanical (adjective) something that is produced or run by one or many machines

migration (noun) the act or process of migration, which is moving from one place or region to another

minimise (verb) to make something as small as possible, or to make something seem less important or valuable than it is

misery (noun) an emotional condition in which one is very unhappy and suffers very much

misunderstanding (noun) a failure to understand something, or another word for a fight or quarrel

mobile (adjective) something that is able to move or be moved easily from one place or position to another

monolingual (adjective) someone who is able to speak, read and understand one language

moral (noun) a lesson about right and wrong learned from a story or event

motorcade (noun) a procession of motor vehicles that occurs for ceremonial or security purposes

mulberry (noun) the berry-like fruit of a shade tree with broad leaves

mural (noun) a large picture painted on or made a part of a wall or ceiling

myth (noun) a story or group of stories that form part of the traditional knowledge of a society. Myths often use imaginative plots and characters to explain how the world began and why nature and people behave the way they do

nightingale (noun) a small bird that lives in Europe and is known for its beautiful song. A nightingale is a kind of thrush

obligation (noun) something that someone should or should not do because of a law or moral principle

off-road (adjective) a type of vehicle used away from streets and highways

outskirts (noun) the edges or outlying areas of a city or town

overcome (verb) to win against or defeat, or to get over or past

overrun (verb) to spread over, to take hold

permanent (adjective) something that is long lasting or built to last for a long time

philosopher (noun) one who studies the nature of life, truth, knowledge and other important human matters

physician (noun) a doctor of medicine, who is licensed to treat illness and injury

pile (noun) a number of things on top of each other, a heap or a stack. For example, a pile of clothes

pitch (noun) a presentation to potential customers to sell a product, or the presentation of a business idea to people who may want to invest in the business

plains (noun) a large, flat area of land without trees

plot (noun) the storyline or order of events in, for example, a story, book, play or movie

popular (adjective) something that is liked or enjoyed by many people

portfolio a range of responsibilities held by a particular group of people; a collection of drawings, designs or other papers that represent a person's work

possession (noun) something that is owned

poverty (noun) the condition of being poor or having a lack of money

precious (adjective) something that is of great worth or value

prefabricated (adjective) something that is fabricated or partially constructed beforehand (of a building or piece of furniture) or manufactured in sections to enable quick or easy assembly on site

pristine (adjective) something that is pure, fresh, good as new or unspoiled and unsullied

promote (noun) to advance or encourage. In advertising, a promotion is a publicity campaign for a particular product, organisation or venture

propose (verb) to suggest a plan of action, or to offer something for the purpose of discussion or thought

prosper (verb) to be successful, thrive or have good luck

quantity (noun) an amount of something

queue (noun) a line, sometimes of people or cars. Often refers to those waiting to be served

quite (adjective) to do something to a somewhat high degree; somewhat, rather

rarely (adverb of frequency) something that happens infrequently, or not too often

reasonable (adjective) showing good sense and clear thinking

recently (adverb) something that happened in the near past, or not too long ago

recycled (verb) something that has been put through a process that allows used things to be reused

refreshments (noun) something that refreshes, such as food and drink

remains (noun) the things which are left when parts have been taken away or destroyed; a corpse; or the ruins or traces of the past

remotely (adverb) to do something from a distance

renovated to restore something to a good state of repair

repurposed (verb) something that has been adapted for use in a different purpose

revival (noun) the act or process of renewing or reviving

royal (adjective) something that is of or having to do with a king or queen, or any members of their family

setting (noun) the surroundings in which an event takes place, the environment. In a story, this would be the environment in which the action happens

share (verb) to receive, use or enjoy together with one or more others

shared (adjective) owned, divided, felt or experienced by more than one person

shuttle (noun) a vehicle or aircraft that travels regularly between two places

shyness (noun) the quality or state of being shy, or not comfortable with other people

silk (noun) a fine, soft, shiny fibre produced by certain insects, or the material made of this fibre

site (noun) the location or proposed location of a town, city, building or event

slightly (adverb) to a small degree or by a small amount; a little

society (noun) the members of a community or group considered together

space (noun) any empty area or place, or a place to live

spirits (noun) a feeling or mood

spoil (verb) to damage or ruin; make unable to be used or enjoyed

stalactite (noun) a rock formation that looks like an icicle and hangs from the roof of a cave. Stalactites are built up from minerals in dripping water

stalagmite (noun) a rock formation that looks like a cone and is built upward from the floor of a cave. Stalagmites are built up from minerals in dripping water

stamp (verb) to mark with a carved and inked rubber or wooden block that makes a design, letters or numbers

subsidies (noun) financial assistance or support provided by any individual, group or government to another

sustainable (adjective) something that can be maintained at a certain rate or level. Sustainable development conserves balance in the environment by avoiding using up all the natural resources

sustainable living (noun phrase) living in a way that meets our need for food, water and shelter, without harming our environment or compromising the availability of essential resources for future generations. To live sustainably we must use less of the Earth's natural resources, replenish what we can and produce less polluting waste

tag line (noun phrase) a catchphrase or slogan, especially as used in advertising, or the punchline of a joke

talented (adjective) having a natural skill or gift in some activity

target market (noun phrase) a particular group of consumers or customers at which a product or service is aimed

terraced (adjective) (of land) having been formed into a number of level areas resembling a series of steps

three dimensional (adjective) having or appearing in three dimensions; having depth as well as height and width. Or, being lifelike and realistic

trader (noun) a person who buys and sells goods, also known as a dealer or a merchant

traditional (adjective) relating to customs and ways of doing things in a particular culture that are passed down from parents to children

translation (noun) when writing is changed from one language to another

treasury (noun) the money of a club, business, government or other group

unspoilt (adjective) not spoiled, in particular (of a place) not marred by development

urban sprawl (noun phrase) the uncontrolled expansion of urban areas

urbanisation (noun) the process by which the population in cities and towns grows as people leave rural areas for urban areas

version (noun) a particular form of something, or a description of events from one point of view

viral (adjective) something that is quickly and widely spread through social media

washroom (noun) a room with washing and toilet facilities, a bathroom or a lavatory

wheelchair (noun) a chair on two large wheels that is used by those who cannot walk

whizz kid (noun) a person who is extremely clever at something

wonder (noun) a thing or event that causes admiration, surprise or amazement

zero-carbon (adjective) causing or resulting in no net release of carbon dioxide into the atmosphere

Irregular verb forms

Infinitive	Present participle	Simple past	Past participle
to be	being	was/were	been
to beat	beating	beat	beaten
to become	becoming	became	become
to begin	beginning	began	begun
to bend	bending	bent	bent
to bite	biting	bit	bitten
to bleed	bleeding	bled	bled
to blow	blowing	blew	blown
to break	breaking	broke	broken
to bring	bringing	brought	brought
to build	building	built	built
to burn	burning	burnt, burned	burnt, burned
to buy	buying	bought	bought
to catch	catching	caught	caught
to choose	choosing	chose	chosen
to come	coming	came	come
to cut	cutting	cut	cut
to dig	digging	dug	dug
to draw	drawing	drew	drawn
to do	doing	did	done
to drink	drinking	drank	drunk
to drive	driving	drove	driven
to eat	eating	ate	eaten
to fall	falling	fell	fallen
to feel	feeling	felt	felt
to find	finding	found	found
to fly	flying	flew	flown
to forget	forgetting	forgotten	forgotten
to get	getting	got	got
to give	giving	gave	given
to go	going	went	gone
to grow	growing	grew	grown
to have	having	had	had
to hear	hearing	heard	heard
to hide	hiding	hid	hidden
to hit	hitting	hit	hit
to hold	holding	held	held
to hurt	hurting	hurt	hurt
to keep	keeping	kept	kept
to know	knowing	knew	known
to learn	learning	learned, learnt	learned, learnt

Infinitive	Present participle	Simple past	Past participle
to leave	leaving	left	left
to lend	lending	lent	lent
to let	letting	let	let
to lie	lying	lied	lied
to lie (down)	lying	lay	lain
to light	lighting	lit, lighted	lit, lighted
to lose	losing	lost	lost
to make	making	made	made
to mean	meaning	meant	meant
to meet	meeting	met	met
to pay	paying	paid	paid
to put	putting	put	put
to read	reading	read	read
to ride	riding	rode	ridden
to ring	ringing	rung	rung
to run	running	ran	run
to say	saying	said	said
to see	seeing	saw	seen
to sell	selling	sold	sold
to send	sending	sent	sent
to sew	sewing	sewed	sewn
to show	showing	showed	shown
to shut	shutting	shut	shut
to sing	singing	sang	sung
to sit	sitting	sat	sat
to sleep	sleeping	slept	slept
to slide	sliding	slid	slid
to smell	smelling	smelt, smelled	smelt, smelled
to speak	speaking	spoke	spoken
to spend	spending	spent	spent
to stand	standing	stood	stood
to steal	stealing	stole	stolen
to swim	swimming	swam	swum
to take	taking	took	taken
to teach	teaching	taught	taught
to tell	telling	told	told
to think	thinking	thought	thought
to throw	throwing	threw	thrown
to understand	understanding	understood	understood
to wake (up)	waking	woke	woken
to wear	wearing	wore	worn
to win	winning	won	won
to write	writing	wrote	written

Grammar

Abstract nouns

Abstract nouns describe things that you cannot see, feel or touch, such as ideas and thoughts. For example:

- happiness, fun, achievement

Adjectives

Adjectives describe nouns and pronouns and allow us to make comparisons. Adjectives add colour and interest to a story, so they are very important in storytelling. Adjectives do not agree with the noun or pronoun they describe. They do not have plural forms. For example:

- These are eerie places!
- That is the most beautiful place I have ever visited.
- She is taller than her sister.

We can use adjectives to make comparisons. To compare two things we use the comparative form (+ er).

To compare more than two things, use the superlative form (+ est).

If an adjective has more than three syllables, add 'more' or 'most'. For example:

- beautiful, more beautiful, most beautiful

Some adjectives have irregular comparative and superlative forms: For example:

- good, better, best

We can use adjectives in different ways to make comparisons. For example:

- This year there were twice as many people here today as yesterday.
- That is the best place I have ever visited.
- It is one of the highest mountains in the world.
- Are there more visitors than last year or fewer? There are many more visitors this year.
- Flying is by far the quickest way of getting to the island.

We can form adjectives with the suffixes -ing and -ed. For example:

- interested, interesting

Compound adjectives are made with descriptive words joined by a hyphen. For example:

- a well-known fairy tale
- a life-changing experience

Adverbs

Adverbs modify (tell us more about) verbs, adjectives and other adverbs. Adverbs can be words or phrases. They describe manner, place and time, including indefinite time.

Examples:

- She runs quickly. (manner)
- They live near a big farm. (place)
- We visited her yesterday. (time)
- My family has recently moved to Singapore. They have lived there since 2020. (indefinite time)

You can use adverbs to compare actions. For example:

- high, higher, the highest

If an adverb has more than two syllables, you add 'more' or 'most' to make comparisons.

Adverbial phrases tell you more about a verb, just like adverbs do. They do not have a verb.

Connectives

Connectives link words, clauses, sentences and ideas when we speak and when we write. Connectives also help to put events in sequence. For example:

- before, after, then, while, when

We use connectives to give explanations, examples, reasons and purpose. For example:

- and, because, or, but, although, therefore, so, so that, such, so as

Pronouns can also help to connect ideas because they refer back to nouns.

We can use connectives to contrast or show the difference between ideas. Use words such as but, though, although, while, unlike. For example:

- Most people know the name Tim Berners-Lee but/although/though they think he invented the internet.
- Cleopatra ruled a huge empire but/although/though she was not liked by all.
- While Cleopatra was famous for her beauty, she was also a skilled royal leader.
- Unlike you, I have not seen the film.

Conditional clauses

First conditional

We use the first conditional if there is a very real possibility that something will happen in the future. For example:

- If you arrive late, you will miss the train. (If + present simple tense + will)

We use the second conditional when we want to say the second thing will only happen if the first part of the sentence happens. For example:

- If she spoke German, she would study in Germany. (If + past simple tense + would)

Zero conditional clauses (with 'if')

We use the zero conditional to say things we know are true and to talk about science facts. For example:

- If you heat ice, it melts. (If + present simple = present simple)

Gerunds

Gerunds are action nouns, that look like verbs. We form gerunds by adding -ing to a verb stem.

A gerund can be the subject of a sentence. For example:

- Swimming is my passion!

(In this sentence the gerund is before the verb.)

A gerund can be the object of a sentence. For example:

- I have stopped reading the news, because so much of it is fake news!

(In this sentence the gerund is after the verb in the main clause.)

After some verbs we can use an infinitive or a gerund. For example:

- I love acting. I love to act.

The following verbs are always followed by a gerund: enjoy, keep, mind, finish, stop.

You can also use gerunds after prepositions of place and time. For example:

- We need to make a decision before advertising the position.

Infinitives

The infinitive form of a verb is a verb that has 'to' in front of it. For example:

- They want to surf this afternoon.

Modal verbs

Modal verbs are verbs that are added to the main verb to express permission, obligation, advice, possibility or ability. Modal verbs do not change form.

Use the infinitive without 'to' after modal verbs:

- can, could: possibility and ability
- may, might: possibility
- must, have to: obligation
- should: give advice, make suggestions
- must: necessity
- may, can: permission
- can, may: make requests
- can't: prohibition

Nouns

A noun phrase is a group of words (without a verb) that makes sense. You can replace the noun with a noun phrase. For example:

- People in the street were queuing to buy the pizzas.

Compound nouns

Compound nouns consist of two nouns.
For example:

- classroom, dishcloth

Phrases

A phrase is a group of two or more words, without a verb. We can make noun, adjectival, adverbial and prepositional phrases.

Prepositions

Prepositions describe location, time and direction. For example:

- in, on, under, at, near, towards, off

Prepositional phrases

We can use prepositions before adjectives and nouns in prepositional phrases.

Prepositional phrases start with prepositions and can include nouns and adjectives. For example:

- She left on the fast train.

Dependent phrases

Some phrases depend on certain prepositions for their meanings. We always use these prepositions after certain adjectives or verbs to make phrases with a certain meaning. The words they depend on can be adjectives, nouns or verbs. The preposition 'for' is used after many nouns and adjectives. For example:

- Adnan is quite good <u>at</u> sailing. (after an adjective)
- Here is some information <u>about</u> natural wonders. (after a noun)
- The country is famous <u>for</u> its volcanoes. (after an adjective)

Some prepositions are always used after certain verbs. For example:

- We have often argued <u>about</u> tourism at this natural site.
- The site needs to be protected from <u>pollution</u> and over-tourism.
- Do you believe <u>in</u> stories like that?

Pronouns

Pronouns replace nouns, so you don't have to keep repeating the noun.

- Subject pronouns: I, he, she, it, you, we, they
- Object pronouns: me, him, her, it, you, us, them

Demonstrative pronouns

Demonstrative pronouns point out a specific person or thing or contact between people and things. For example:

- this, that, these, those

Indefinite pronouns

Indefinite pronouns refer to people in a general way. For example:

- some, one, anyone, someone, everyone, no one

Quantitative pronouns

Quantitative pronouns indicate an indefinite quantity. For example:

- some, any, none, one, much, many, little, few

Reciprocal pronouns

Reciprocal pronouns are used when two or more people are doing the same thing. For example:

- each other (for two people)
- one another (for more than two people)

Relative pronouns

Relative pronouns connect clauses in sentences. They can be used with prepositions. For example:

- to whom, from whom, with which, on which, from where

Note: If a word is followed by a noun, it is an adjective, not a pronoun.

Quantifiers

Quantifiers describe quantities. They tell us *how many* or *how much* there is of something.
For example:

- all, some, any, no, less, few, most, both, plenty of, enough

Relative clauses and pronouns

Relative clauses are clauses that begin with relative pronouns, such as who, that, which, whom, whose, where and why. These pronouns link the clauses.

We use 'who' to refer to people.

'Whom' is quite formal. Many people would use 'who' or 'that' in this sentence.

Clauses can be defining or non-defining. You can remove a non-defining clause and the sentence will still make sense. For example:

- This is the house where she used to stay. (defining clause)
- Maria, whom you met last week, is my best friend. (non-defining clause)

Register

Register is using language directly according to who you are speaking or writing to. For example, in a formal register you would write:

- It's impressive what Sean has managed to achieve.

In the less formal, or more casual register, you might write:

- Cool, right?

Reported and direct speech

Direct speech

We use this to quote the actual words that someone spoke. Direct speech is always inside speech marks (' and ').

Reported speech

We use reported speech to say what someone said. In reported speech we change the pronouns, the tense of the main verb, demonstratives and any adverbs of time. The word order changes too.

For example:

	Direct speech	Indirect speech
statement	'I have fish and chips,' said the woman.	The woman said she had fish and chips.
question	'Do you know this word?' the teacher asked.	The teacher asked if I knew that word.
command	'Bring your gym clothes tomorrow,' the captain told us.	The captain told us to bring our gym clothes the next day.

When you need to change direct speech to reported speech, do the following:

- Change the word order.
- Look at the verb tenses. Go back one tense.
- Look at the nouns. Change them to pronouns.
- Look at words that express time and change them if necessary. For example:
  this = that
  now = then
  today = that day

Sentences

Sentences have:

- a subject (the person doing the action)
- a verb (the action).

Most sentences also need:

- an object (the thing the action happens to).

The subject and object of a sentence are usually nouns.

Verbs

Active and passive voices

We can use the active voice or the passive voice of verbs to describe present, future and past actions.

For example:

Tense	Active voice	Passive voice
Simple present	They play baseball in summer.	Baseball is played in summer.
Simple present continuous	They are playing baseball on the field.	Baseball is being played on the field now.
Future	They will force us to share the room.	We will be forced to share the room.
Simple past	The visitors enjoyed the meal.	The meal was enjoyed by the visitors.

To form the passive, use the verb 'to be' in different tenses + past participle.

Remember that some past participles are irregular. See the list on pages 161–62.

The passive voice is used:

- when you don't need to say who does the action
- if you don't want to say who the subject is.

Future forms

There are different future forms:

To describe plans and arrangements that have already been made. For example:

- We are going to visit friends this evening. (use going to + verb stem)

To make predictions. For example:

- The sport will appeal to young people.
- I shall be famous one day! (use will/shall + verb stem)

To describe future arrangements with fixed dates. For example:

- The new school year starts on 7 September. (use the present tense)

Past continuous tense

We use this tense to describe an action that was in progress while something else was happening. For example:

- As I was getting on the train, I dropped my phone.

To form this tense: verb 'to be' in the past form (was, were) + present participle (-ing).

Past perfect tense

We use this tense to describe an action in the past that was completed before another action in the past. (Use the past perfect to describe the earlier action and the simple past to describe the other, later action.)

To form this tense: use had/has been + the past participle (-ed).

Past simple tense

We usually form the simple past tense -ed. For example:

- play = played
- dance = danced

Some past tense verbs have irregular past tense forms. For example:

- go = went
- take = took

Look at the list of irregular past tense verbs on pages 161–62 if you are not sure.

Present continuous tense

We use this tense to say what is happening at the moment, as we are speaking. For example:

- I am watching the other passengers on the train.

We also use this tense to talk about future arrangements. For example:

- We are going to Prague next month.

To form this tense: verb 'to be' (am, is, are) + present participle (-ing).

Present perfect tense

We use this tense to describe a recent or unfinished action that we did in the past and that we are still doing or hope to do in the future.

To form this tense: use the verb 'have/has' + past participle.

Present perfect continuous tense

We use this tense:

- to describe something started earlier and is continuing in the present time
- to emphasise the duration of something.

To form this tense: use have/has been + the present participle (-ing).

To form a question: change the word order.

To form a negative: add 'not' after the word 'have'. For example:

- I have not been working.

Remember that if a verb ends in -e, you have to drop the -e before you add -ing.

Present simple tense

We use the present simple tense:

- to talk about habits and routines
- to describe people
- to talk about things that are always true.

For example:

- He/she wears school uniform.

The verb for the third person singular ends in -s.

Punctuation

A B C	Capital letters are used for the first letter of a name, country, place, nationality, days of the week, months of the year or language.
.	A full stop shows the end of a sentence. It may also be used after initials, e.g. N.J. Hill and abbreviations, e.g. B.B.C.
,	A comma shows a short pause that separates parts of a sentence or words in a list.
( )	Brackets show extra information or an explanation which is considered less important.
" " or ' '	Speech marks show words that are spoken directly. They are also used around the title of films and books. Speech marks may be double – " " or single – ' '.
'	An apostrophe is used when two words are contracted. It is also used to show possession, e.g. it's Bill's.
-	A hyphen is used when two words such as compound nouns are joined together, e.g. son-in-law.
?	A question mark is used at the end of a sentence which asks a direct question. It is also used for requests. Can you buy some milk, please?
:	A colon is used to show that something is coming next, e.g. a list.

Pronunciation

Great Barrier Reef
Gretel
griot
guy

H

Halong Bay
Hansel
Harbor Rio de Janeiro
hare
Harry Potter
Hawaiian
hemisphere
hereditary
heritage
hippies
historical
holiday
honoured
hustle

I

Ibn Sina
illustrate
imaginery
industries
infectious
influencer
infographics
intelligent
interview
Inuit people
inventor
Ira Gershwin
Iraq
irrigation
island
Italian

J

Jamail
Japan
Jason
Joe
Johannes Gutenberg
Jonas
Jonno
journal
journalist

K

Kalpana Chawla
Karlu Karlu
Kenya
kitchen
Korea

L

lamp
language
Lara
lava
layers
Lee
legislation
Leonardo da Vinci
Leonardo DiCaprio
Leonie
Leslie
lift
lyrics

M

magazine
Malaysia
Mandarin
Manuela
Marco Polo
Marie Curie
Maryam
Masdar
mathematician
mechanical
Meena
Meera
Melissa
messy
metropolis
Mexican
Michelle Obama
Middle East
Mike
Milan
Miles
million
mining
misery
mobile
modules
Mohandas (Mahatma) Gandhi
Mongol Empire
monkey
monolingual
Montgomery
moral
mosquitoes
mother tongue
Mount Everest
mountain
mulberry trees
municipality
museum
myth
mythology

N

nails
Nelson Mandela
New Zealand
niece
nightingale
Nikki
Nikolas Tesla
noise
noodle
Northern Ireland
Northern Lights

O

obligatory

P

pandemic
Parícutin
Paris
parliament
Patricia
Paul
peaceful
Pedro
Penny
permanent
Peter
petrol
Philippines
philosopher
physician
pitch
Plato
podcast
police
Polish
politician
pollution
poppies
portfolio
Portuguese
possession
poverty
prang
prefabricated
preserve
prince
princess
Princess Diana
printer
pristine
Puerto Princesa Subterranean River National Park
Puerto Rico
Punta Ventana

Q

Queen Latifah

R

racial injustice
Raj
red herring
Red Riding Hood
reggae
religious
resistance
revival
rhythm
river
robot

Rosa Parks
royalty
ruins
rural
Russia

S

school
scientists
scuba diving
sculptor
sea
Sean
segregated
Selena Gomez
Serengeti plains
Shafika
shelf
shocking
Sichuan
silk
ski slope
sky
slippers
snow
Socrates
solar
sparkled
spirits
sprawl
stalactites
stalagmites
Stella
Stockholm
strawberries
stripes
stunning
subsidy
succession
supplement
sustainable
swan
swearing
Switzerland

T

Table Mountain
talented
Tanzania
Tariq
techno
technology
television
terraces
The Netherlands
theatre
ticket
tiger
Tomas
tortoise
tourism
transport
Treasury
Trevor Noah
trilingual
trilogy
trunk
Tunku Abdul Rahman

U

underground
United Arab Emirates
United Kingdom
unspoilt
urban
urbanisation

V

vegan
vegetation
Venice
Victoria Falls
Vietnam
villagers
viral
virtually
voice
volcano
vulnerable

W

Wangari Maathai
waterfall
West Africa
wheelchair
whizz
wings
women's suffrage movement
wood
woodcutter

Y

Yi

Z

Zambia
zero-carbon emissions
Zimbabwe

Reading for enjoyment

Do you want to find out more about some of the topics you have learned about? Reading a range of fiction and non-fiction books for enjoyment will help build up your vocabulary in English. Use a dictionary to look up some words you don't know, but remember you don't have to look up every word you're not sure about because you can try and work it out from the context. It's a good idea to keep a reading journal, so you can record what you have read and what you thought about the book.

Here are some suggested fiction and non-fiction books you might like to try.

Third-party resources referred to in this section have not been endorsed by Cambridge Assessment International Education.

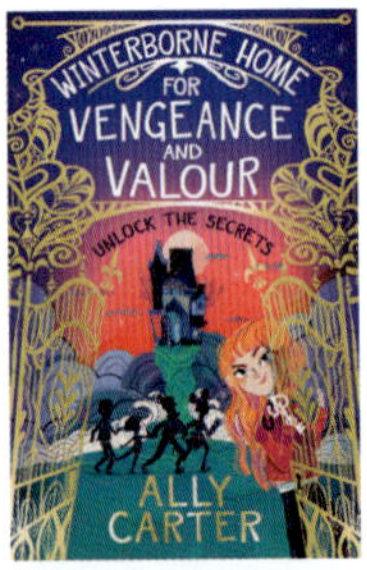

Winterborne Home for Vengeance and Valour (ISBN: 9781408357378) by Ally Carter, Orchard Books

Planet Omar: Accidental Trouble Magnet (ISBN: 9781444951226) by Zanib Mian, Hodder Children's Books

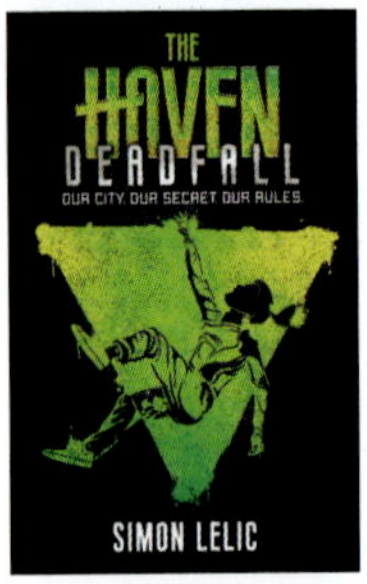

Deadfall: Book 3 (The Haven) (ISBN: 9781444947649) by Simon Lelic, Hodder Children's Books

My Awesome Guide to Getting Good at Stuff (ISBN: 9781526362681) by Matthew Syed, Wren & Rook

Go Big: The Secondary School Survival Guide (ISBN: 9781526362353) by Matthew Burton, Wren & Rook

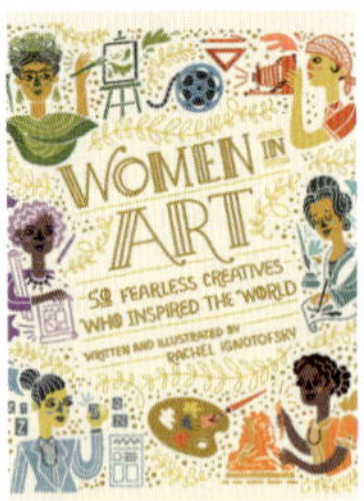

Women in Art: 50 Fearless Creatives Who Inspired the World (ISBN: 9781526362452) by Rachel Ignotofsky, Wren & Rook

Toto the Ninja Cat and the Great Snake Escape (ISBN: 9781444939453) by Dermot O'Leary, Hodder Children's Books

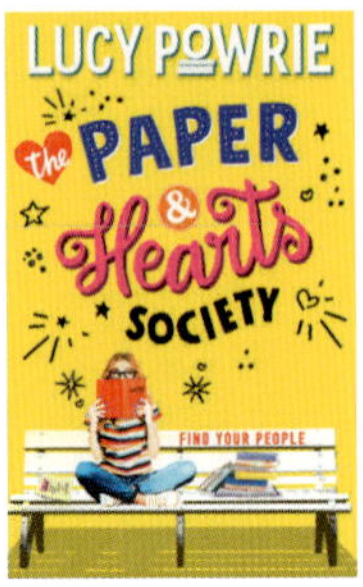

The Paper & Hearts Society Book 1: Find Your People (ISBN: 9781444949247) by Lucy Powrie, Hodder Children's Books

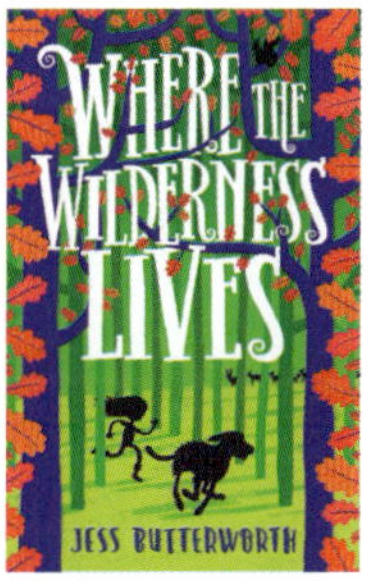

Where the Wilderness Lives (ISBN: 9781510105508) by Jess Butterworth, Orion Children's Books

Fire Boy (ISBN: 9781444954685) by J M Joseph, Hodder Children's Books

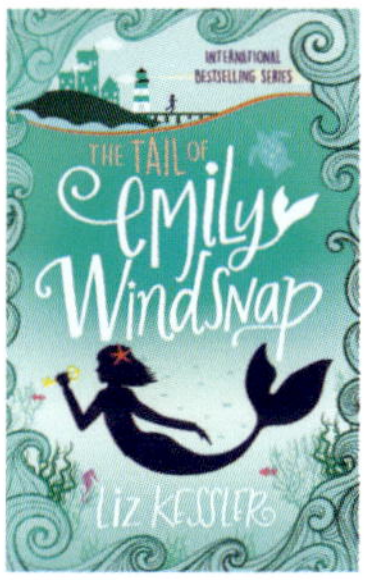

The Tail of Emily Windsnap (ISBN: 9781444015096) by Liz Kessler, Orion Children's Books

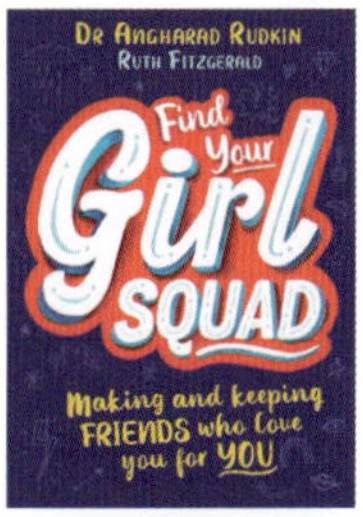

Find Your Girl Squad (ISBN: 9781526362506) by Dr Angharad Rudkin and Ruth Fitzgerald, Wren & Rook

The Boy at the Back of the Class (ISBN: 9781510105010) by Onjali Q Rauf, Orion Children's Books

This Book Will (Help) Cool the Climate (ISBN: 9781526362414) by Isabel Thomas, Wren & Rook

Boot: Small Robot, Big Adventure (ISBN: 9781444949360) by Shane Hegarty, Hodder Children's Books

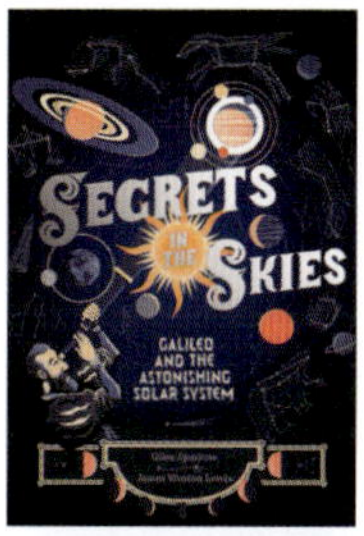

Secrets in the Skies (ISBN: 9781526360014) by Giles Sparrow, Wren & Rook

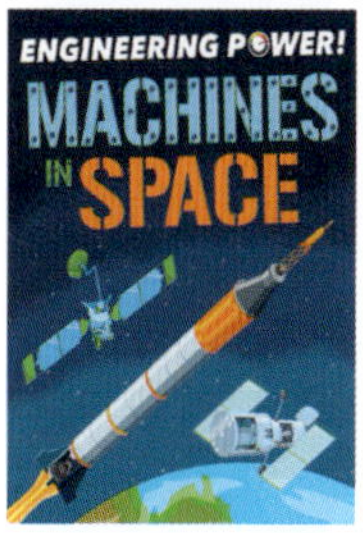

Engineering Power! Machines in Space (ISBN: 9781526311801) by Kay Barnham, Wayland

Stand Against: Prejudice (ISBN: 9781445168210) by Izzi Howell, Franklin Watts

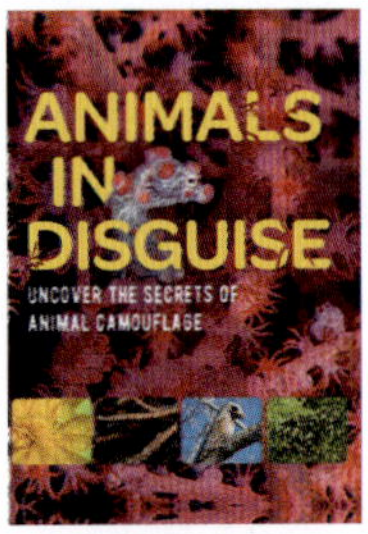

Animals in Disguise (ISBN: 9781526312143) by Michael Bright, Wayland

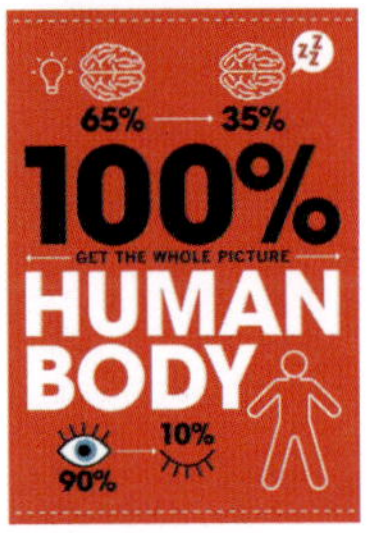

100% Get the Whole Picture: Human Body (ISBN: 9781526308139) by Paul Mason, Wayland

Stand Against: Poverty and Hunger (ISBN: 9781445167398) by Alice Harman, Franklin Watts

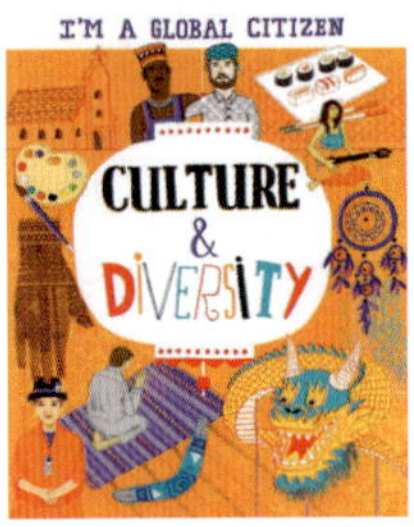

I'm a Global Citizen: Culture and Diversity (ISBN: 9781445163987) by Georgia Amson-Bradshaw, Franklin Watts

Space Science: STEM in Space: Science for Rocketing into Space (ISBN: 9781526308115) by Mark Thompson, Wayland

Space Science: STEM in Space: Science for Exploring Outer Space (ISBN: 9781526308467) by Mark Thompson, Wayland

Cats React to Science Facts (ISBN: 9781526311160) by Izzi Howell, Scholastic Inc.

Endangered Wildlife: Ocean Life (ISBN: 9781526310002) by Anita Ganeri, Wayland

Acknowledgements

The Publishers would like to thank the following for permission to reproduce copyright material.

Every effort has been made to trace or contact all copyright holders, but if any have been inadvertently overlooked, the Publishers will be pleased to make the necessary arrangements at the first opportunity.

Text credits

p.145 'I am prepared to die' by Mandela, Nelson; **p.146** Coronavirus outbreak FAQs: what you can and can't do, © Crown Copyright. Contains public sector information licensed under the Open Government Licence v3.0.

Photo credits

r = right, *l* = left, *b* = bottom, *t* = top, *m* = middle

p.7 © Monkey Business/stock.adobe.com; **p.8** © Drobot Dean/stock.adobe.com; **p.9** *l* © Sondem/stock.adobe.com; *r* © Ilya/stock.adobe.com; **p.10** © Rh2010/stock.adobe.com; **p.11** © Ajr_images/stock.adobe.com; **p.12** *t* © Phpetrunina14/stock.adobe.com; *b* © Auremar/stock.adobe.com; **p.13** © SilverScreen/Alamy Stock Photo; **p.14** © Bluedesign/stock.adobe.com; **p.15** © Bluedesign/stock.adobe.com; **p.16** © Ekaterina Belova/stock.adobe.com; **p.17** © Ekaterina Belova/stock.adobe.com; **p.18** © Elnur/stock.adobe.com; **p.20** *t l* © Joserpizarro/stock.adobe.com; *t r* © Jovannig/stock.adobe.com; *b l* © Fotohansel/stock.adobe.com; *b r* © RnDmS/stock.adobe.com; **p.21** © RnDmS/stock.adobe.com; **p.22** *t l* © Monika/stock.adobe.com; *t r* © Jamesteohart/stock.adobe.com; *b l* © Josunshine/stock.adobe.com; *b r* © Henktennapel/stock.adobe.com; **p.23** *t* © Maya/stock.adobe.com; *b* © Andrey Zhuravlev/stock.adobe.com; **p.24** © Viacheslav Iakobchuk/stock.adobe.com; **p.27** © Toltemara/stock.adobe.com; **p.28** *l* © Trekandphoto/stock.adobe.com; *r* © Aleksandr Zholobov/stock.adobe.com; **p.30** © Victoria/stock.adobe.com; **p.31** © Victoria/stock.adobe.com; **p.32** 'Drone-delivered holiday home – prediction from Samsung SmartThings Future Living Report, published February 2016.'; **p.33** 'Drone-delivered holiday home – prediction from Samsung SmartThings Future Living Report, published February 2016.'; **p.35** *l* © Susan Waldron/stock.adobe.com; *r* © Jeffery Edwards/Shutterstock.com; **p.36** *l* © Ostap25/stock.adobe.com; *m* © FrankBoston/stock.adobe.com; *r* © Diversepixel/stock.adobe.com; **p.37** © FrankBoston/stock.adobe.com; **p.38** *t l* © Jehsomwang/stock.adobe.com; *t r* © Yuliyanna/stock.adobe.com; *b l* © Ake/stock.adobe.com; *b r* © Fergregory/stock.adobe.com; **p.39** © Editonepankaj16/stock.adobe.com; **p.40** *t* © Archivist/stock.adobe.com; *b* © Archivist/stock.adobe.com; **p.41** © Dmitriy Trubin/Shutterstock.com; p.42 © Quickshooting/stock.adobe.com; p.43 *t* © Quickshooting/stock.adobe.com; *b* © Orensila/stock.adobe.com; **p.45** © Destina/stock.adobe.com; **p.48** *l* © Valmedia/stock.adobe.com; *r* © Valmedia/Shutterstock.com; **p.50** *l* © Maciej Es/Shutterstock.com; *r* © Victor Moussa/stock.adobe.com; **p.51** © Matiasdelcarmine/stock.adobe.com; **p.52** © Stanciuc/stock.adobe.com; **p.55** *l* © Nongnut Moijanghan/Shutterstock.com; *r* © Annamei/stock.adobe.com; **p.56** *t l* © HstrongART/stock.adobe.com; *t r* © Pio3/Shutterstock.com; *b l* © Krakenimages.com/stock.adobe.com; *b r* © 2p2play/Shutterstock.com; **p.60** © EtiAmmos/stock.adobe.com; **p.61** *t* © Tashatuvango/stock.adobe.com; *b* © EtiAmmos/stock.adobe.com; **p.62** © FotoCorn/stock.adobe.com; **p.63** © FotoCorn/stock.adobe.com; **p.64** © Voinsveta/stock.adobe.com; **p.66** *t* © Guardian News & Media Ltd 2020; *b* © Tide; **p.67** © Jack Dempsey/AP/Shutterstock; **p.68** © Torychemistry/stock.adobe.com; **p.69** © Torychemistry/stock.adobe.com; **p.70** © Michail Petrov/stock.adobe.com; **p.71** © Michail Petrov/stock.adobe.com; **p.72** *t l* © Nomad_Soul/Shutterstock.com; tr © Fortune-stock/shutterstock.com; *b l* © Michelly Rall/Stringer/Getty Images; *m* © Andocs/Shutterstock.com; *b r* © Alfa27/stock.adobe.com; **p.74** © Antonioguillem/stock.adobe.com; **p.75** *t* © Will/stock.adobe.com; *b* © Luckybusiness/stock.adobe.com; **p.76** © Santypan/stock.adobe.com; **p.79** © George Taylor/Everett Collection/stock.adobe.com; **p.82** © Jarno Holappa/123 RF.com; p.85 t © Magicbeans/stock.adobe.com; *b* © Vchalup/stock.adobe.com; **p.86** © Abasler/stock.adobe.com; **p.87** © Abasler/stock.adobe.com; **p.88** *t l* © Lukas/stock.adobe.com; *b l* © Mandritoiu/stock.adobe.com; *t r* © JoseLuis/stock.adobe.com; *b r* © Biletskiy Evgeniy/stock.adobe.com; **p.89** © Andreanita/stock.adobe.com; **p.90** *t* © Mirko/stock.adobe.com; *b* © Philippe/stock.adobe.com; **p.91** © Philippe/stock.adobe.com; **p.94** *t* © Aitormmfoto/stock.adobe.com; *b* © Alexandre Patchine/stock.adobe.com; **p.95** *l* © Evagattuso/stock.adobe.com; *r* © Whitcomberd/stock.adobe.com; **p.96** © Evagattuso/stock.adobe.com; **p.97** © Evagattuso/stock.adobe.com; **p.98** *l* © Balate Dorin/stock.adobe.com; *m* © Superjoseph/stock.adobe.com; *r* © Maygutyak/stock.adobe.com; **p.99** © Maygutyak/stock.adobe.com; **p.100** © Balate Dorin/stock.adobe.com; **p.102** *l* © Slepitssskaya/stock.adobe.com; *m* © Rafael Ben-Ari/stock.adobe.com; *r* © Daniel Prudek/stock.adobe.com; **p.103** © Slepitssskaya/stock.adobe.com; **p.105** *t l* © Bradleyvdw/stock.adobe.com; *t r* © Gracethang/stock.adobe.com; *b l* © Visionsi/stock.adobe.com; *b r* © Sergiy/stock.adobe.com; **p.106** *t l* © Grafik-Komputerowy/stock.adobe.com; *t m l* © Amir Zainorin/Artwork title: George/Medium: postcards and pins on wall/Year: 2010; *t m r* © EQRoy/Shutterstock.com; *t r* © Catwalker/Shutterstock.com; *m l* © Chrisdorney/stock.adobe.com; *m r* © Serato/Shutterstock.com; *b* © Nosyrevy/stock.adobe.com; **p.107** © Vkilikov/stock.adobe.com; **p.108** © Drserg/Shutterstock.com; **p.112** © Silvy78/stock.adobe.com; **p.113** © Neftali77/123 RF.com; **p.114** © Ukko/Shutterstock.com; **p.115** © *The Star*, Malaysia; **p.116** *t* © Funfunphoto/stock.adobe.com; *b* © Hppd/stock.adobe.com; **p.117** © Hppd/stock.adobe.com; **p.118** © KnowBeingInTime/stock.adobe.com; **p.119** *t* © Diegobib/stock.adobe.com; *b* © KnowBeingInTime/stock.adobe.com; **p.120** *t l* © NASA Archive/Alamy Stock Photo; *t m* © Wendy Stone/Corbis Historical/Getty Images; *t r* © Historic Collection/Alamy Stock Photo; *b l* © Natata/Shutterstock.com; *b m* © Yury Zap/stock.adobe.com; *b r* © Johan10/stock.adobe.com; **p.122** *t* © Mubus/stock.adobe.com; *b* © Arenaphotouk/stock.adobe.com; **p.123** *t* © BestForYou/stock.adobe.com; *b* © Carballo/stock.adobe.com; **p.124** © Tartila/stock.adobe.com; **p.125** © Paul Maguire/stock.adobe.com; **p.127** © Iakov Filimonov/Shutterstock.com; **p.128** *l* © Masdar; *r* © Anna Ostanina/Shutterstock.com; **p.129** © Anna Ostanina/Shutterstock.com; **p.130** *t* © SolisImages/stock.adobe.com; *b* © Rawf8/stock.adobe.com; **p.131** *t* © SolisImages/stock.adobe.com; *b* © Pavlo Glazkov/stock.adobe.com; **p.132** © Volha Stasevich/Shutterstock.com; **p.133** *t* Laurian ghinitoiu; *m* © Volha Stasevich/Shutterstock.com; *b* © Oliver Foerstner/Shutterstock.com; **p.134** © Oliver Foerstner/Shutterstock.com; **p.135** *l* © Marina Kryuchina/Shutterstock.com; *r* © Torsten Pursche/stock.adobe.com; **p.136** *t* © Mark/stock.adobe.com; *b* © Viacheslav Iakobchuk/stock.adobe.com; **p.137** © Viacheslav Iakobchuk/stock.adobe.com; **p.139** © JackF/stock.adobe.com; **p.140** *l* © Monkey Business/stock.adobe.com; *r* © Makieni/stock.adobe.com; **p.141** © Miniloc/stock.adobe.com; **p.142** © Goran Jakus/stock.adobe.com; **p.144** © Johan10/stock.adobe.com; **p.145** *t* © Alessia Pierdomenico/Shutterstock.com; *b* © Poco_bw/stock.adobe.com; **p.146** *t* © Romolo Tavani/stock.adobe.com; *b* © Robert Kneschke/stock.adobe.com; **p.147** © Romolo Tavani/stock.adobe.com; **p.148** © Olgavolodina/stock.adobe.com; **p.152** © Anton Gvozdikov/stock.adobe.com; **p.153** © Anton Gvozdikov/stock.adobe.com; **p.155** *t* © Malickim/stock.adobe.com; *b* © Volha Stasevich/Shutterstock.com